SEX, SATAN, AND JESUS

RICHARD HOGUE
SEX, SATAN, AND JESUS

Broadman Press/Nashville, Tennessee

© Copyright 1973 • Broadman Press
All rights reserved

4353-19 (hardback)
4253-20 (paperback)

ISBN (hardback): 0-8054-5319-9
ISBN (paperback): 0-8054-5320-2

Library of Congress catalog card number: 73-86668
Dewey Decimal classification: 241
Printed in the United States of America

Photographs by
Gilbert Productions, Inc., Denver

To my beautiful Spirit-filled wife,
Marilyn,
God's "one worth waiting for"

Foreword

"If it feels good, do it!" This one statement seems more than any other to catagorize the prevailing attitude of sexual behavior in this generation.

In a time of revolutionary newness and change, nothing is facing more radical revision than sexual standards. Things which were once thought to be right are today totally rejected. God's law of sexual purity is considered a joke. From doctors to educators, philosophers, ministers, and entertainers, we are told "everything goes . . . tear down the restraints . . . do your own thing . . . make your own rules."

Behind this new outlook on sex is a force beyond that of mere human strategy. Indeed Satan himself is having a heyday. Moving as he always has to plot and destroy man's relationship with God, he is using sex as never before.

Caught in the very middle of this barrage of change and revolution is the Christian—young and old. Who does he listen to? Who does he believe? What really is true? Where does he turn as he faces a new society with new goals, new directions, new technology, new educationalism, new ideas, new morals and the same old adversary who has been seducing men away from God's law since Eden—Satan! Where is the answer for that Christian who longs to keep himself sold out to his Master yet must survive this generation in which he finds himself?

This book is written to that Christian. God has something to say about today, its pressures, its changes, its enemy. The things he has to say can—if you will allow them—give you victory over every temptation Satan can throw at you, especially that of sex!

Contents

1. What in the World Is Going On? 13
2. Pressure to Tolerate Everything 19
3. Temptation to Rebel 32
4. Meet Public Enemy Number One 45
5. If You Love Me, Prove It! 73
6. What's So Great About Being a Virgin? 85
7. Let Him Put It All Together 95
8. "The Morning After Blues" 117
9. Admit It, Quit It, and Forget It 133
10. "Get On Your Fatigues" 142
11. It's Worth Waiting For! 155

SEX, SATAN, AND JESUS

1

What in the World Is Going On?

While I was speaking in New Orleans recently, a girl told me she shared sexual intercourse with anyone she could because it was her way of rebelling against the "hypocrisy of today." She said, "I am against moral injustices, against the repression of the female, and the institution of the church." This, she said, "is my way to demonstrate." Unbelievable, you say? No, not unbelievable at all. It is just a part of a generation that has opened itself up to anything and everything in the area of sex.

A few months ago, one of the network evening news shows reported that along the east coast of the United States, people were shocked to hear that police were breaking up fifth- and sixth-graders involved in sex rings to and from school.

Some experts say that 60 percent of the women and 80 percent of the men have lost their virginity before marriage. British author Malcolm Muggeridge, writing in *The New Statesman,* observed that sex "permeates" every corner and cranny of life, from birth to the grave. American mores, he says, are "drenched if not submerged" in sex. We live in a sex-saturated society, and it seems that you cannot escape.

The Kinsey reports, published some twenty-five years ago, revealed that half of all husbands had cheated on their wives at one time or another, over one-third of all men had engaged in at least one overt act of homosexuality, and that one in six of all rural boys had experienced sexual contact with *animals*. That was long before the "sexual revolution" of the sixties and seventies.

In Dayton, Ohio, a thirteen-year-old girl wrote a newspaper to ask for information about how she could handle her boyfriend who, as she says, "only wants my body for a sexual instrument." In Southern California today the so-called "swingers" or "wife swappers" are a growing part of a culture that says anything goes with sex.

And a lot must be going, because there are 400,000 illegitimate children born each year in the United States. This number represents an amount of one birth in twelve, and up to one in two among all births in central city black ghettos. This is not a racial statistic. The rate would be much higher among affluent whites except for abortions (1,500,000 per year), greater availability of contraceptives, illegal adoption (much easier among whites), and "shotgun" marriages among young girls who are pregnant before the marriage ceremony.

Also, sex-related crimes show an alarming increase in this generation. The FBI reports that in the decade that ended in 1970 the incidence of rape in the United States increased by 120 percent to 37,500 reported cases per year, with an estimated three out of four acts going unreported due to personal reasons. The probable United States annual total of rapes, then, is around 150,000. On top of that, an estimated one million cases of child molestation occur each year in the United States.

Across America, venereal disease is fast becoming pandemic. Syphilis among teenagers and young adults is up more than 250 percent since 1960, according to the Communicable Disease Center in Atlanta, Georgia. There are 650,000 cases of venereal disease reported yearly in the United States. Just since 1900 various forms of syphilis have killed approximately 100 million people. During that same period in the United States, it is estimated, syphilis has killed more than three million babies and more than one million adults, according to *VD: Facts You Should Know,* by Andre Blanzaco, a consultant at the Atlanta Communicable Disease Center. The American Social Health Association says that gonorrhea now is pandemic and threatens the health and welfare of the next generation.

Every place we go around the country, I constantly am amazed as I speak in high schools and colleges at how frustrated principals and administrators are in fighting this problem of venereal disease. These principals constantly ask us to help in any way we can; and you can understand their alarm because VD has doubled in the last five years. It looks as though it will double again by 1975.

Dr. Warren Ketterer, Chief of Venereal Disease Control for the California Public Health Department, told a seminar in San Francisco that in some urban sections of California at least 20 percent of all high school students will contract venereal disease before they get their diplomas. In 1970, the California State Department of Public Health said in a report that "one in ten Californians under twenty-five will have VD each year, and this age group will have half of all reported cases." Statistically, every sixteen seconds another American is infected with VD, every other one a youth under twenty-five.

The April 23, 1973, issue of *Newsweek* reported that a former car salesman now is building hotels across Europe and possibly behind the Iron Curtain, with the sole purpose and business being (in the words of *Newsweek*) "booming sex hotels" with a capital investment of 9.5 million dollars, much of which has been invested by several Americans. These hotels are springing up to offer prostitution with class or, as they say it, "sex with a heart."

Another thing which is exploding in this generation is homosexuality. A few months ago in Dallas, Texas, in a gay liberation march, hundreds of people shouted the slogan "Gay Is Good," and these were not just young people, but housewives, businessmen, and even one eighty-year-old woman.

Most reliable sources estimate that there are around ten million homosexuals in America alone. About 2½ million of these are full-time male homosexuals, about one million are lesbians (or female homosexuals), and about six million are bi-sexuals; and in the last few years, about 10,000 individuals have had operations to change their sex. According to the *National Observer,* there are hundreds of exclusively gay bars, clubs, and bathhouses. The *National Observer* continued in the April 14, 1973 issue, to say that, "Two homosexual newspapers now have a combined circulation of nearly 60,000 people." The entire gay liberation movement has come right out in the open. Even a dictionary has been written called the *Queen's Venacular.*

What in the World Is Going On?

Complete sexual freedom is now the "in thing," to make way for today's philosophy that says "if it feels good, do it." According to this viewpoint, if you believe in keeping your sexual purity before marriage, then you are completely out of it. In fact, one professor on a Houston television talk show just a few weeks ago said that if you are a virgin, "you are in the most ridiculed minority in America."

In fact, to sit and listen to some late night talk shows, you would think that only people that have severe insecurities would ever wait until marriage for sex. There are constant jokes about divorce and marriage, but tragedy is no joke. The Family Service Association of America says that "family breakdown is fast reaching epidemic proportions and now ranks as America's number one social problem."

Just in the 1970's alone, there have been over two million divorces in the United States. According to the Census Bureau, fifteen million Americans have been through a marriage breakup, and that does not count about 100,000 desertions each year. There are 2,000 divorces every day in the United States, and most of these are due to sexual incompatibility. As NBC News recently reported, more than one in three marriages now end in divorce in the United States. In fact, every forty-three seconds there is another American divorce. Among teenagers, the problem is worse. About 40 percent of all teenage marriages involve premarital pregnancy, and about one-half of these end in divorce.

The tragedy is that behind these so-called hard facts are the lives of millions and millions of people who are either directly involved or in the families of those directly involved. There is little wonder that this coming generation has shown an outright intimidating attitude for the institution of marriage, because many of these people have come from broken homes. Many of these kids have had to live with parents whom they knew really did not love them or want them.

Life magazine said no other civilized nation comes close to the United States in its divorce rate, and it's really little wonder. I have seen married men around this nation in airports and motels who have been totally captivated by the sex-orientated society we live in.

Any newsstand today that you walk into in any airport will have an entire array of books complete with every type of infidelity, homosexuality, sadism, or any other type of weird, mixed-up perversion that you can imagine.

Sloppy, illicit, perverted, weird, free, premarital, extramarital sex—that's the world in which we live.

According to the Mayor's Citizens' Antipornography Commission in New York City, "a veritable floodgate of obscenity has opened up in the last few years in the form of obscene pocket books, magazines, and greeting cards, to such an extent that it is unbelievable." It staggers your mind to realize that between 500 million and one billion dollars is spent annually on hard-core pornography.

Long lines of pleasure-seeking customers caused one recent hard-core pornographic film, entitled *Deep Throat,* to net over one million dollars in one New York City theater alone.

There is no way to get around it. There is no way to avoid it. The "sexual revolution" is here.

2

Pressure to Tolerate Everything

Leaving Miami, Florida, late one night to go back home to Houston, I sat down on the airplane. In the seat next to me were about five or six copies of the same issue of *Fortune* magazine. As I picked up a copy, I noted the cover advertised an article by Edward Faltermayer called "Youth After the Revolution." In the article, Faltermayer says, "The most noticeable change among high school students in the past ten years is the acceptability of the open display of affection in corridors. Formerly, this would have drawn a scolding or worse from a member of the staff, and girls would have feared for their 'reputations.' Today, many say that what others do is their business. Says one boy at California's Woodside High School, 'It's uncool to say it's wrong.' " As we travel around the country, I must admit Faltermayer's observations are very true.

Recently, I was in Brownsville, Texas, to do an assembly in the high school. As we drove up, we were amazed that all over this campus were couples not just holding hands, but embracing, kissing, and petting. One couple which I almost had to untangle to get in the front door could have done little more than they were doing even if they would have been in the backseat of their car.

In San Diego, California, during the lunch breaks, it was not unusual at all to see couples on the grass around the high school making out like crazy.

It floors you how openly sex is accepted today. As you start looking for a reason for the "acceptability" of this new sexual behavior, you find yourself discovering not only a new sexual standard, but a completely new outlook on any type of standards in almost every area of life. As *Look* magazine's senior editor said, "We are seeing the death of the old morality. Conditions are changing so fast that the established moral codes have been yanked right from out of our hands. No single authority rules our conduct. We are in the midst of a moral crisis because the great majority of Americans who want to try to live moral lives no longer can be certain what is right and what is wrong."

Only a few years ago, there were some definite rights and some definite wrongs. Today, the only authority that seems to determine what is accepted is man's own lust and pleasure. That's the type of philosophy which men justify in the name of psychology. For example, according to a widely held view, Freud believed that man's problems all basically come from sexual frustration. He is supposed to have believed that everything started and ended with sex. This view holds that the entire human race is motivated mainly by pleasure and that society keeps man from really fulfilling this drive of his erotic desires. Supposedly, if we could take all of the repression away, man would be wonderfully happy. There is no real purpose to mankind's existence on the earth. There is no God, no real direction, and so everything can go. Psychology is invoked as supporting such beliefs.

As a result, society has lessened its repression and in fact, accepts sex with little restraint. Many people are fulfilling every sexual drive that can be dreamed up. Yet we are still living in a world with frustrations and problems; everything isn't "just all right."

As Boris Sokoloff says in his book *The Permissive Society* about the philosophy attributed to Freud, "There is no God and so all is permitted." This philosophy has influenced every major campus, many of our churches, and many of the intellectual leaders of the world. So it only makes sense that a generation nurtured with this prevailing philosophy has rejected any idea of an ultimate authority—a God who has the right to call man to sexual purity. In fact, God has come off as the villain. The very idea of God trying to tell man what to do! The outlandish audacity of God to tell man there are some things that are definitely wrong and to set a standard for morality beyond man's right to alter with his actions. In so many words, we've told God, "My sex is my business. I'll do what I want to do."

The prevailing attitude in society is that what a person does behind his bedroom door is his business—his alone. Not even God has the right to intervene. It is this type of philosophy which has led to a frequent abandoning of the sexual standards put forth in the Bible. Man seemingly has accepted any form of sex as legitimate. We wonder why a change like this could so overpower a generation until you realize that change comes in cycles. First the change is tactitly approved, perhaps criticized but still approved. Then it is tolerated ("Since we can't do anything about it anyway"—people say). Then finally it is accepted ("Well, everyone is doing it"). Only a fool would say we have not accepted a new sexual standard of behavior today.

Look at homosexuals alone. There you can see the change. Laws have been changed. Already eight states have legalized homosexuality. Social scientists and educators are increasingly saying that society will just have to be more understanding with homosexuals. We are asked to accept homosexuality as just another life style. You can see the change in politics. As the *National Observer* reported, the 1972 Democratic National Convention responded to gays' demands for a strong gay rights platform plank, yielded enough to adopt this platform statement: "Americans should be free to make their own choice of life-styles and private habits without being subject to discrimination or prosecution." The *National Observer* also says that young people are the rank and file of the gay liberation movement.

In one Maryland high school, a clique is preparing to demand administration recognition of the school's gay students organization. The University of Minnesota's student-government president until recently was a law student whose election campaign featured two posters wryly alluding to his homosexuality. One said, "Put yourself in Jack Baker's shoes," and showed the candidate scroonched up effeminately, wearing women's high heels. Today, where once society totally rejected homosexuality as a valid life-style, most people say it is very "in" to be "tolerant" and "understanding".

The *National Observer* says that before gay liberation only a few occupations tolerated obvious homosexuals. But gay lib has encouraged authors, journalists, teachers, librarians, clergymen, scientists, engineers, government personnel, GIs, and countless college students to come "out of the closet." While most gay organizations are still college-oriented, gay professionals are infusing the movement with an unprecedented self-assurance. Declares Jean O'Leary, an outspoken lesbian leader, "Homosexuality is a valid life-sytle. We are no longer going to be in the closet feeling guilty and queer." The label "homosexual" came to connote yesterday's timidity, says the *National Observer*. "Gay" denotes today's defiant pride.

It is this type of defiant pride that is evident in every area of the sex behavior. The things we are reading for entertainment denote the change of acceptance to give new sexual standards. *Cosmopolitian* magazine came out recently with twelve rules for a successful affair. One teenage magazine which is in most high school libraries around the country said, "If you are old enough to think seriously about having intercourse, you are not too young to make your *own* decisions." The magazine continued, "Sex is stimulation, and satisfying experiences are as normal as breathing."

Marriage is being looked upon today as a light-hearted commitment of two people who want "to play house for a while and then can break it up and go their separate ways." The average person is being swamped with this new philosophy. Even the basic make-up of society tends to this continual evolution of changing sexual patterns.

Where only a generation ago, 75 percent of America was rural, today 75 percent of America is urban. What this means is that we live in a time of more peer pressure than the world has ever had to face. In this generation, young people and adults are constantly with other people. Think about the life-style of the average teenager who wakes up in the morning, gets on the bus, goes to school, spends the day, gets back on the bus, comes home, maybe does one hour of homework, grabs a meal, goes out with his friends that night, comes in to grab a few hours of sleep so he can get on the bus the next day. He is constantly and continuously with the group. In fact, he almost looses his own thoughts and feelings to those of the group. He finds himself going along with ideas and acts because "everyone else is doing it." In a day when everyone is free and can "do his own thing," very few really are different from what is happening in their own area of friends. The group in many cases becomes the mind which makes the decisions.

In San Diego, California, a young boy in junior high came up to talk to me after our services one night. As we began to talk, even before we had arrived at the real thing that was haunting him, he kept saying "I really didn't mean to do it. I really did not want to do it." As he finally unveiled the story, he said he had been at some friends' house who were supposed to have only a little party. When he got there, many people were dancing, some of the guys were back in the back smoking some grass, but in his words, everything seemed to be all right. As the party progressed, couples would be chosen to go into the bedroom and have intercourse in front of everyone else. As the night went on, he found himself watching, enjoying, and finally participating in what was going on. I honestly believe he really did not want to do it. But, if you don't think the pressure is great, you are crazy. So where does a person turn—who does he listen to, what is right, what is wrong? He is being bombarded as never before from every side, but, where does a person turn?

From the very beginning of history, there have been two great institutions which God ordained to train a person in the way he should live, relate, and act sexually. Those two institutions were first the family and then later the church, but where are they today? Many of them have gone over to the enemy side of the fence. They have deserted. They have committed treason. Many parents today are a part of the problem instead of the cure. We now have the most permissive parents the world has ever known. So when Junior listens to his dad telling him to "wait until marriage," it is hard to listen. Why? Because Junior knows that his dad is not being faithful to mom inside the marriage, so why should Junior be faithful outside of marriage?

We hear that the young people have gone to the dogs sexually. Well, it is time we shared the blame. They don't deserve all the credit. It is not the young people that have commercialized and exploited the sexual drive. It is not the young people that keep the X-rated movies in business. They can't even get in until they are eighteen. Many times it is the same adults who support adult movies that blame the kids for having dirty minds.

Young people receive their sexual standards (or their lack of them) from their parents. But in the family which many teenagers grow up in, there is no love between the parents. They see nothing but quarreling and bickering every time they come home. So instead of looking toward marriage with respect and honor, many young people almost hate the word. They say, "I am not going to wait until marriage for sex. I am going to know *if* I cannot live with someone before I get married and *have* to live with that one. So at a time when sexual emphasis is at an all-time high, the platform of parental guidance has collapsed.

One night we were in Los Angeles on Sunset Strip when a big, black Cadillac pulled up to the curb right in front of us. Out came an entire herd of kids—really a bunch of freaks. I walked over to them and said, "Where did you get the car?" One of the guys said, "It belongs to my old man." I was amazed. Here was a limousine with a chauffeur driving it around and out of it had come some of the freakiest kids you could ever imagine. I said, "You mean your dad had his chauffeur drive you down here?" "That's right," he said, "That's right." I asked him why he did that. The kid looked at me and said, "They are swapping, and they wanted us to get out of the house." What that means is that up in the Hollywood Hills some place, there are his parents and several other couples changing wives for a night of sexual pleasure. In essence, they simply sent the kids down on the strip to do the same thing. It is amazing how parents have dropped the standard in the area of sex.

The magazine *Human Behavior* says that "friends and peer groups" are far and away the largest source of sexual knowledge. Kids are learning on the streets what God intended to be taught at home. Sometimes, it is a good thing because many homes set a poorer example than the streets.

As Faltermayer said in *Fortune*, today's young people have grown up in a time where the primary influence in upbringing increasingly shifted from adults to contemporaries. There is little wonder the family is having the trouble it is when you realize the attack the normal family is under.

Parade magazine, in a nationwide survey, asked the question: "Is the American housewife happy?" Though there were some exceptions, the general answer was *no*. The place of the father is being constantly dragged down. No longer is he that authority that God made him to be in the Scriptures. Many television shows and comic strips show the father as a lame-brained idiot who can barely make it home from the office without the help of his wife, who busily settles every problem, manages the finances, quiets the protesting children, and still has time to send him off to the office with a pat on his head. But even though we're living in a time when the family is under attack, the family and parents especially cannot escape their responsibility to be the example with the force of guidance in their child's sexual life.

Most of the cause of homosexuality can be directly linked to the family. Homosexuality comes primarily from a home without a loving, father-led marriage. Today's emphasis on "unisex" and the abandoning of responsibilities linked to male and female roles are possible factors that add to homosexual behavior. In his book *Homosexuality: A Psychoanalytic Study*, Irving Bieber reports that out of 106 homosexuals he studied, not one had a normal relationship with his father. And Bryan Magee, in his book *One in Twenty,* concludes that, "Over and over again, it is found that a homosexual person has had an intense relationship with the mother and a deficient one with the father."

Dr. Charles W. Socarides, a New York psychiatrist, argues in the *International Journal of Psychiatry,* that homosexuality is not an innate abnormality, but rather "acquired behavior." He writes, "Homosexuality is based on the fear of the mother and the aggressive attack against the father. The homosexual is not only afraid of women, but he also harbors the deepest aggression against men."

Many parents are naïve at the point of sex in the life of their children. One mother, talking about a sex column in a Dayton, Ohio, newspaper, said, "I do not think kids of fourteen know anything about sex." How stupid—how utterly stupid can some people be?

At the same time, while parents are not doing their part in sex guidance, look at the church. And I speak as a man who loves the church and as one who can realize that many churches and pastors take very strong stands for the sexual standards God has ordained in the Bible. But the world seldom sees these churches or hears these men. Instead they see stories about things like the Church of the Holy Apostle in Manhattan, which recently became the first Episcopal parish to hold regular Sunday services primarily for homosexuals and to perform "holy unions" of gay couples. Recently, one Protestant denomination ordained a declared homosexual into its ministry. The ministerial candidate was asked by one of his examiners,

"Do you regard homosexuality as a gift from God and a good gift?" In answer he replied, "I regard all sex as a gift from God and a good gift." To another question concerning his attitude about marriage, he quickly responded, "I think love between any two people is beautiful and should be celebrated. I know two men or two women can share such love." In less than one hour, the final decision was made. Representatives of nineteen San Francisco Bay area churches of the United Church of Christ approved the ordination of an acknowledged homosexual into their ministry.

Entire "Christian professing" churches now exist— complete with liturgy, choirs, and marriage ceremonies—which are comprised almost exclusively of male and female homosexuals, pastors included. There are gay churches in several major metropolitan areas. Think of it—even from inside churches, there are cries of, "Lessen the sexual standards." We hear, "What is wrong with sex before marriage or sex outside the biblical guidelines?" And supposedly, there are "preachers" who ask this question.

So where is a person to turn, who is he to believe—society . . . the family . . . the church? Seemingly they are all openly accepting this new morality with all its sexual ramifications. To compound the problem of this changing philosophy and attitude of sex, the misuse of sex and the perversion of it and the temptation to yield readily are available to those who will participate.

In movies, in plays, in books, in every possible advertising gimmick, sex is the key word. Even advances in science and medicine have made the acceptability of this changing sexual standard more agreeable with us. One mother in Lubbock, Texas, told me, "I give my teenage girls birth control pills. I don't care if they have sex; I just don't want to be embarrassed by a pregnancy." Abortions are now almost available upon demand. The car has become a motel room on wheels. Advance techniques of warfare bring pressure to have sex when you can, for tomorrow we may all be blown away. All of these things lend weight to the unbelievable acceptance of a complete change in the way people view sex.

At a junior high school in Louisville, Kentucky, we were filming some publicity for an upcoming crusade. In a classroom discussion, a student said, "You can get anything you want in the way of drugs or sex in our school." How readily available sex is to any and every age group.

This is why our entertainment has turned to having no sex standards. Anything is acceptable. A new film with Marlon Brando reputedly shows open sexual intercourse, oral sodomy, and other types of sexual indulgence. This type of sin is so accepted that *Time* magazine carried a story of the film and gave it front cover attention.

The *National Observer* reports that, thanks to gay liberation, meeting compatible homosexuals is no problem in most big cities. Gay movies and plays are now shown in legitimate theaters. There are gay travel agencies, resorts, beauty shops, dating services, and even groovy "pen-pal" clubs.

It is staggering to realize the fantastic changes that have taken place within just the last few years in the area of sex. But more staggering is the unbelievable acceptance which it has received. Why? What is the reason? Where do the changes come from? We could blame it on philosophy which says if it feels good, do it. We could blame it on education which simply tells us that we are only another animal, or on entertainment which exploits the sexual drives of every age group. We could blame it on parents who committed treason, on pressure to go along with whatever is happening. We can blame it on nature. But the real culprit is getting away with murder in the area of sex and going completely unnoticed. The real culprit behind the change, behind the philosophy, behind the entertainment, behind the pressure, behind the unbelievable acceptance—the real culprit is Satan.

3
Temptation to Rebel

Her defenses were down. She had petted, but not like this. She had never really wanted to go all the way before, but now she did. Was it love? It must be. She had never felt like this before.

Karen grew up in Sunday School and church. She was not a tramp. She was *not* cheap. She could be anybody's nice girl next door.

She knew all the "thou shalt not's" including the seventh. But in a moment, she threw it away. Why? Was it the mood? The moment? The man? No. It was none of these things. Karen had a debate with the devil and *lost*. Oh, she never knew it was Satan. Never. In fact, if someone would suggest that as the reason she shed her virginity like an old coat, she would have laughed it off. But that is exactly what happened. It is exactly what Satan has tried to do since the very creation of man. He knows God's law for sex better than we do, and he knows sex is an area which, in many lives, he can use to put that barrier between God and man.

Now, you must realize Satan did *not* force Karen to have intercourse with the guy, but the temptation, as Satan dealt directly with her own selfish lust, came straight from

Temptation to Rebel

the mind of the devil. Satan in his cleverness and shrewdness knew better than to openly attack Karen, so he simply dealt with her through suggestion. "You're old enough to make your own decisions; no one will ever know. Besides, this is a new day." It is a new day, and because it is Satan has an easier time than he ever had tripping people up with the misuse of sex.

The temptation of sex without marriage, or course, did not begin with this generation. But the pressures to yield to this temptation are both new and deadly.

So *what* if a person yields? so what? Who is he going against? The world certainly does not demand sexual purity in its ideas, its philosophy, or its life-style. So there is no conflict with the world. In fact, the only authority which calls a person to wait until marriage for sex and that sex be restricted to marriage, the only authority that makes that demand is the Word of God. So the temptation to go against God's written law for sex comes as a form of rebellion against God—sin. Satan has led us to say, in so many words, "God, get out of my mind, out of my life, out of my sex, and leave me alone. I will do whatever *I* want to do." Man has taken a new authority, an authority which says, "I will be my own judge; I will be my own authority; I will live the way I want to live; the only thing that matters is what I want."

There was a time when even the greatest skeptic would say there had to be an authority of life beyond man's own mind, but not now. Man has finally made himself God. So a part of this attack by man on the authority of the Word of God and the right of God to control his life shows itself in the new sexual freedom of this generation. God says "Thou shalt not commit adultery," and man says, "I will if I want to." In essence, Satan has led man to make his own rules, to ignore what God has to say.

The devil comes and says, "What difference does a slip of paper make? You love this boy, you love this girl." Then he says, "You are going to marry anyway, why shouldn't you go all the way with each other?" What could sound more reasonable than this? How can you deal with that type of argument? This is what happens to most young people and adults who get lost in the modern jungle of sex pressurers. God has some clear-headed, intelligent things to tell us about how to use our sex drive, but we are so busy listening to the devil that we don't hear God.

"The devil made me do it" is no joke. Satan himself is the enemy. He is trying everything he can to destroy this generation with sex and, though the pressure may come from a thousand different directions, Satan is the problem. And you will never get victory until you realize there is a real devil who is "out to get you." Anytime you listen to only one side of an argument, you are bound to come up with a lopsided opinion, and that is exactly what we are doing with sex today. If the world would listen to God, we would hear God say, "For this is the will of God, that ye should abstain from fornication" (1 Thess. 4:3). But the devil does a snow job on us. He convinces us that giving our bodies away is really a virtuous act. That is one of the devil's oldest tricks. If he can convince us that we are doing something good by doing something bad, then he has us hooked. And today, he has done that on a grand scale.

Another line of Satan's is, "But if you love one another, aren't you already married in the eyes of God?" But the

Bible says NO! "Keep clear of all sexual sins so that each of you will marry in holiness and honor and not in lustful passion as the heathen do" (1 Thess. 4:3-4).

The person who says "Why wait until marriage?" really says that he wants your sex and body more than he wants your happiness. But worse than this, he may also be saying that *all* he wants out of a marriage is sex. If your love demands sex now, you probably don't have much of a platform for a stable marriage. You had better have a lot more than sex to share in your marriage because nine-tenths of a marriage is spent *outside* of the bed.

One thing which we do not seem to realize is that sex does not constitute a marriage. So many people we talk to around the country feel that the only thing that they must do to be married in the eyes of God is to supposedly "love" each other—and have a desire to share intercourse. Then Satan fools them into believing that the intercourse is okay with God since they "love" each other. They rationalize that God sees their love and that makes them married in his eyes. But that is a lie of HELL.

You see, marriage is a commitment. It is a structure of authority which was ordained and instituted of God in the Garden of Eden.

Marriage is not something that just "evolved" through the reasoning and gradual civilization of man. Rather, marriage was ordained by the Creator, Almighty God. It is holy and sacred to God. The sin of lust is more fully understood and detested when you realize how right and holy the proper way of sex is to God.

In the book of Genesis, God sets up this divine institution of marriage. In fact, Jesus says in Matthew 19:4-6, "Have ye not read, that he which made them at the beginning made them male and female, and for this cause shall a man leave father and mother, and shall cleave to his wife: and they twain shall be one flesh?" "What therefore God hath joined together, let not man put asunder." Those are the words of Jesus.

Now, admittedly, marriage is a physical union; but it is a "divine institution." You must realize that in the original Greek New Testament the word "cleave" which Jesus used means to be joined together. It is talking about sex. In other words, when God made Adam and Eve in the Garden of Eden, he gave them perfect sex. He made sex to be the highest expression of this marriage, an expression that cannot be duplicated by any other relationship in life. In the Bible, the meaning of human marriage is awesome. You realize that God is so interested in the institution of sex and marriage that in drawing an analogy between Jesus and the church, he says, "The church is the bride of Christ." You realize throughout the Scriptures that it is God who started marriage in the first place. He is the one who set down the laws to constitute marriage so that man and woman could live together in perfect peace, happiness, and joy. At creation, the God of this universe showed it was not good for man to be alone, and he created woman as a wife for him. He blessed them and said, "Be fruitful, and multiply, and replenish the earth." (Gen. 1:28)

There is no way to get around it. God ordained and created the institution of marriage. Marriage is then a physical relationship which began in the mind of God. Marriage is a spiritual contract which God has placed high above the laws of human society. Once it is bound in heaven, that contract is unchangeable. And Jesus said that except for fornication by one of the partners or the death of one of the partners, marriage in the eyes of God is unbreakable (Matt. 5:32).

Marriage is serious; marriage is permanent; marriage is for keeps. So if you start using the institution of marriage as an excuse for your sex, you had better ask yourself some questions. Am I really willing to make a lifetime commitment to this person? If you are the woman, you should ask yourself: Am I willing to be submissive to this man and honor him as my husband as God demands? If you are the man: Am I willing to love her and provide for her and care for her for the rest of my life? Satan loves nothing better than to take something precious to God like marriage and sex and use them as tools to destroy man. Why? Because Satan hates God, and the only way he can get to God is to destroy what God loves most—MAN!

Another trick of the devil is to tell you that sex sins hurt only your body and your mind, not your relationship to God. Wrong again. Sexual sin causes a deterioration of the soul and a separation from God. To think that you are not hurting anything if you don't get the girl pregnant and if you don't get or give a disease is childish and devilish thinking. Paul told young Timothy, "Whoever says that he belongs to the Lord must turn away from wrong-doing" (2 Tim. 2:19). "Flee fornication" (1 Cor. 6:18). "Flee also youthful lusts" (2 Tim. 2:22). "To avoid fornication, let every man have his own wife, and let every woman have her own husband" (1 Cor. 7:2). He gave these commands not just because of the physical, but because of the spiritual. "Do not be deceived, neither fornicators, nor idolaters, nor adulterers, nor effeminate, nor homosexuals . . . shall inherit the kingdom of God" (1 Cor. 6:9-10).

Any law of God's that you break is bad. But sexual sin involves much more. Many times the misuse of sex is a sin against yourself; but beyond that it is a sin against that one you share sex with as well as an outright sin against God and his law.

Satan knows that, which is why he often uses "religious" people to lead other people away from the real laws of God concerning sex. In the 1972 edition of the *U. S. Catholic,* Father Henry Fehren said, "The Church's historic position that homosexuality is immoral has been based on misinterpretations of stray biblical texts written for another age and culture and on a vague, unproved natural law." How in the world "this man of God" could ignore the graphic description of both male and female homosexuals in Romans 1:6-28 is beyond my wildest dreams. And how he could possibly find God's denunciation of homosexuality throughout the Scriptures as "vague" is unbelievable to me.

And yet, it really is not. Satan has had his cronies down through history constantly trying to get people to go against God's established laws for sex. However, the Scriptures declare unapologetically that homosexuality is against the basic design of God's natural law. If you are honest, there is no way to deny those passages.

Today, it is a common theme of writers to glamourize homosexuality and free love. Everyone likes to picture the broad-minded virtues of the jet set swingers against the narrow-minded stuffiness of the church and the parsons.

They leave the impression that the people who have the most fun are those who follow no rules except their own feelings. What a lopsided picture. Anyone who believes this has failed to look at the misery that always follows in the wake of lust.

Never excuse the Prodical Son, in the Bible or in yourself. The Prodical Son always ends up in the pig pen, and it is time that we faced that. If we don't face it with our minds, we will end up having to face it with our experience. God says, "The man should give his wife all that is her right as a married woman, and a wife should do the same for her husband" (1 Cor. 7:3). That means that the sex part of marriage is a great thing. God gave it to enjoy. When we give each other sex in the marriage bed, we are giving the most joyful gift in the world.

Today, some believe we should give sex to anyone who happens along. This idea reads like a lot of fun in a drugstore pornographic book that describes the joys of sexual abandon in warm details. But those who try it find out that it reads a lot better than it lives. When you live that way, you have to wake up and live with the results of it. And that isn't so much fun.

A couple came to see a preacher friend of mine. They had been married about ten years and about to get a divorce. "My wife just doesn't trust me," John said. "You don't trust me, either," the wife said. Both admitted that they had never trusted each other. Then she blurted out the sordid story of their premarital sexual experiences. As a result of these, they have lived with ten years of mutual suspicion of each other. Whenever there was tension, one of them would bring up the past.

Imagine that for ten years. Each knew the other to be an experimenter, and they were always afraid the experimentation still was going on. After hearing that story, the devil usually says, "But I am different." "What is wrong for one person may not be wrong for me. I am smarter than to let that sort of thing bother me." But most of the young men and women we've talked to around this country by the hundreds who have had experience with heavy petting or premarital sex relations say the opposite. First, they get a lot of fun out of it; then they start hating themselves; then they start hating their partners; then they start being embarrassed and ashamed. Finally, they break up and become enemies.

Even if some couple manages to live through premarital sex and goes ahead and gets married, the premarital sex will often lead to frigidity after marriage.

A beautiful young model was saved in one of our Atlanta crusades. As my wife began to deal with her, she found out that her marriage was just about to break up. The problem was frigidity. Every time they tried to have intercourse, she simply refused because she felt guilty about a premarital experience she had with her husband.

God worked this out when both of them got saved. Jesus is always the answer. He can, if you will let him, overcome any point of trouble you are facing.

What God says about sex goes for everyone. There are no exceptions. If you walk off the top of a ten-story building in downtown Houston, you are going to fall down, not up. And it doesn't matter how much you think you are going to fall up.

A city school teacher brought a rabbit to school to show her first grade children. They were delighted with the bunny and asked all kinds of questions. Finally, someone asked if it was a boy or a girl. The teacher was a little frustrated and had to confess that she really did not know. Then one little girl came up with a very democratic solution. "We will vote on it," she said. This kind of thinking characterizes so much of our modern life. But it misses the point. There are some things that do not depend on anybody's vote. Whether the majority is for them or against them is beside the point.

But why does God make such rules? They are so hard to follow. They go against all our biological inclinations. Well, it is not because God is a power-hungry dictator who gets a kick out of making up rules for you to follow. It is because God loves you as a Father, more than you love yourself, that he tells you the rules about sex. And contrary to popular opinion, God's rules are rules *for* sex, not against. God won't stand by and be silent while you foul up your life. God has been around a long time. He has seen the results of thousands of lives wrongfully using sex—the heartaches, the shame, the loneliness, the broken homes. God wants you to have the happiest life you can. And he knows that requires complete sexual purity. He wants you to have the best life, the abundant life. That is why he requires you to wait until marriage for sex within the bounds of marriage.

Another way the devil gets to many Christians is by saying through the old voice of compromise, "Just don't go all the way." That sounds reasonable, so most people are quick to say, "Well, I didn't go all the way." But they forget that married people pet before they have intercourse, and that anytime you pet, the same thing is likely to happen. Once you have started, there is a chain reaction, not just mental, but biological. Do not pet with a person unless you intend to go all the way. It will happen probably in spite of your best intentions. The brain usually loses its final shootout with the sex urge. Don't kid yourself into thinking that you are different; that it can't happen to you. Those are the famous last words of thousands of intelligent young people.

Every time I talk with a young couple who have messed around sexually, I try to find out why it happened. They all say the same: "Well, we never meant for it to happen. We promised each other a thousand times that we wouldn't. But one night we were parked, making out, petting pretty heavy, and all of a sudden we had gone all the way. We got up. We felt dirty and cheap; but it was too late." That is why God says not to mess around with it. Stop while you can. "It is best to be married, each man having his own wife and each woman having her own husband, because otherwise you might fall back into sin" (1 Cor. 7:2). God knows that Satan is just waiting for that perfect moment to move in and destroy your life.

Jesus said, "I say unto you that anyone who even looks at a woman with lust in his eyes has already committed adultery in his heart" (Matt. 5:28). He is telling us that the thought of lust produces the act of adultery, and if you let the thought of lust live in your mind and in your fingers as you explore someone's body in the dark, sooner or later it is going to happen, whether you think so or not. Any thought you hold in your mind for very long will eventually take charge of your actions.

Then Satan comes across with this wonderful lie: "As long as no one gets hurt, what does it matter?" As long

Temptation to Rebel

as no one gets hurt. Now, there is a joke. Any time you mess around sexually outside of God's law of sex, you hurt yourself, and for sure you hurt the one with whom you have sex. Even if no one knows, even if you do not get VD, you give up your purity and you take the purity of someone else. There is no way that a sex act outside of the laws of God will not hurt someone.

Every Christian psychiatrist I have talked to has told me there is no way to determine the mental if not the physical damage that the misuse of sex can cause. Habits of intercourse, petting, homosexuality, masturbation, all are like dynamite in the brain. We must realize that sex is not some toy to be played with at will. Instead, it was given as a gift of God to be enjoyed to its fullest within the confines of marriage. In marriage, sex is given to the man and the woman. That in itself rules out homosexuality. Sex was designed to give overt expression to the real and genuine love for man and his wife, a love which is not just a physical love for her body but a love which is born within his soul.

When sex is used for another purpose or in any other way, it is used against the will of God. When man rebels and misuses sex, he will, without a doubt, suffer for his sin. "Whosoever committeth adultery with a woman lacketh understanding, he that doeth it, destroyeth his own soul" (Prov. 6:32).

Practically everyone has heard the story of Sodom and Gomorrah. The entire plain around Sodom and Gomorrah, including the cities, crops, and everything that lived, was destroyed by fire because of the grievous sexual sins and other vices of the inhabitants. The men of Sodom and

Gomorrah were so perverse sexually that they would even rape other men (Gen. 19:4-9). In fact, read the entire detail of the account for yourself and see what God really thinks about homosexuality.

God has some very plain and level-headed things to say about sex—and he expects man to listen and obey. Any time man refuses, he is going against the Word, and will, of one who loves him more than he even loves himself. And he is surrendering to the temptation of one who simply wants to destroy him. So wise up. Listen to God!

4

Meet Public Enemy Number One

It was an unbelievable, tremendously beautiful tropical garden setting—a paradise. There was nothing any one could have desired or wanted that was not there. In the middle of this Utopia, God placed a perfect human being. He had everything: tremendous health, fantastic good looks, a brilliant mind, abundant wealth in natural resources all around him. He had everything going for him.

But as he looked through this garden, this paradise, ate the fruit, saw the animals, fellowshipped with his Creator, deep within his life there was a longing, a dissatisfaction. He was just plain lonely.

There was no other human being around to talk to or be with, to share his dreams with, no one he could love. He was *alone*. The Scripture says, of course, that God realized the condition of man, and although he had given man everything in the world, even though he had put him inside of paradise and made everything go his way, made him the ruler over his entire creation, God said, "It is not good for man to be alone. I will make a companion for him"—someone to fulfill him and be his partner (Gen.

2:18). Then the Bible says that God put Adam to sleep and performed the first surgery. He took out one of Adam's ribs and used it as the basic substance to create the most beautiful creature in all of God's creation, woman.

When Adam woke up and saw her, he knew instantly what God had done, and he said with great excitement and joy: "This is bone of my bone, flesh of my flesh. She shall be called Woman, because she was taken out of man" (Gen. 2:23). And God said, "Because of this, a man shall leave his father and his mother and shall cleave unto his wife and they shall be one flesh" (Gen. 2:24).

Think of it, God had just performed the first wedding. Here at the opening of the world, God ordained marriage. Since that moment in history, there has never been a couple who had more things going for them to have a happy life and marriage. They just flat had it made. A fantastic "Employer," all the security in the world, no inlaws to mess with, everything was just right. And yet, it is amazing that in just a short time they were evicted (their home was repossessed) and kicked out of the garden. Adam lost his job; he lost his security; he failed in his marriage; he failed his employer; he failed his wife. Think of it. He lost everything. And Eve was a failure, too. She failed her husband, hindered him in his job instead of helping him. She was an influence in the wrong direction. They were both driven from this fantastic Utopia and never again was man to know this ultimate paradise.

There is little doubt about the fact that they both argued. They continually blamed each other for being kicked out of the Garden. Their children grew up in a miserable atmosphere of struggle, hard work, frustration, and bitter disappointment.

Here was a man who in a moment was stripped out of his wealth and security, removed from his job as boss of this world, and made to begin a sharecropper's existence, to eke out a scarce living in the fields. The world became his enemy instead of his paradise. The earth, instead of being covered with fruits and trees, was filled with thorns and thistles (Gen. 3:18). Life became a horrible tedious struggle.

On top of all that, as if life was not bad enough, Adam and Eve saw their own children turn into selfish, disobedient kids. One even murdered the other.

Adam and Eve lived to see their children involved in every imaginable evil. As you read the Bible, you see their children turn to perversion, blood-lust, rape, and murder. They cheated, fought, and stole. In fact, in the early part of the Scripture, you find the descendants of Adam were involved in every possible type of vice. And yet, they had everything to begin with. Why? Why in the world would such a successful beginning come to such a horrible end?

All the old answers that we would give do not fit. One philosophy after another tells us that if man could only find the "perfect" woman, all his problems would be solved. No one could have been more perfect than Eve. She was the most beautifully perfect woman that ever lived, and Adam was the most perfect specimen of a man. Others say that everything would be terrific if the world could have great social security with a perfect ecological balance. Adam and Eve had all of this—plus they had a live, daily relationship with God. But they blew it all. Why?

There is one thing I forgot to tell you about the Garden. Located in the middle of the Garden was one tree called the Tree of the Knowledge of Good and Evil. And God, who had designed this Garden, created the man, and placed him in the middle of it, had given the entire Garden to man except that one tree. God said: "Adam and Eve, this entire place is yours, but do not eat the fruit of that tree, because if you do you will die" (Gon. 2:17).

Now there was nothing wrong with the tree. The tree itself was not evil. It was not filled with some poison. The thing that made the tree deadly was that it was a symbol of God's authority and protection and provision for man. God was saying: I have given you everything in the world you could ever possibly want. All I want you to do is simply love me and obey me. But God was also saying, by putting the tree in the garden: I am not going to cram my will down your throat. I am going to give you the right to make your own decisions. That is why I am not going to remove this tree from the Garden. You have the right to choose to rebel against me and eat the fruit, but you will pay the consequences.

There was one more character who was to enter this paradise at the beginning of man's existence in the world. He is introduced in the opening verse of the third chapter of Genesis. The Bible says, "Now the serpent was more subtle than any other beast of the field which the Lord had made." This serpent was not in the form of a snake. In fact, as you get into the original language of the Scripture, you realize that the word "subtle" means that he was very graceful, beautiful, and lovely. Even the word "serpent" means something shiny and bright. (Some people feel the serpent may have been Eve's pet.) The Scripture says that this beautiful, graceful, fantastic, gorgeous creation, the serpent, came to the woman to tempt her. Just to let you in on a secret, it was not actually the serpent

Meet Public Enemy Number One 49

who tempted Eve. Instead, it was Satan who had taken control of the body of the serpent as an easy way to get to Eve.

Satan's position in the plot was this. Because of God's love for man and because of the relationship that God wanted to have with man, and because of Satan's hatred of God and the things of God, his design was to destroy man, who was the ultimate creation of God. Now, Satan is no idiot. There is certainly no doubt about that.

When he came to Eve to tempt her to rebel against God and eat the fruit of the tree, there was no doubt he had done his homework.

As always, Satan was a master of timing. He waited for the perfect moment. He even knew the exact plan to use. He had studied out the one to be tempted. He realized that man had been given authority over the woman, and that woman was to obey the man, her husband. So instead of coming to Adam to get him to sin, he came to Eve first. If Adam had sinned and led Eve into sin, she would have been innocent, because she would simply have been obeying her husband. So, Satan came straight to the woman. He had to do it right; he could not blow this first opportunity. She might not have given him another chance. So at the exact right time Satan begin to deal with her mind. Probably he placed thoughts like: "Well, what's so different about that tree?" "Why is God so hung up on that tree?" "That fruit does not look any different than any other fruit." Satan probably had begun to work on Eve for days to tempt her thoughts, to place doubts in her mind. Probably he placed thoughts like: "Well, what's up blowing her out of the garden with it.

He is unbelievably clever, extremely wise and cunning. He did not come to Eve and dogmatically say, "God is a liar. You are not going to die." Rather, he simply came and began to question. Carefully, he designed the doubts in her mind. The very first word he said to Eve was, "Has God said you shall not eat of every tree of the garden?" He began to question the word of God. And she said, "Oh, yes, we can eat from every tree in the garden except that one right over there in the middle." She said to the serpent, "God said that if we eat of that tree, we are going to die!" And Satan deceitfully and carefully said, "You won't *really* die." Satan is so smart, so clever. He is so brilliant, and so destructive.

Satan immediately attacked the one single command God had given them. That one single thing God had asked them *not* to do, Satan wanted them to disobey. He tried to make God look like a creep and a liar and he said, "Now, Eve, the real truth is the fact that God knows that if you eat of that tree, then you really will know what is going on. In fact, you will be just like God." In essence, he was saying, "Eve, God is so selfish—he really does not want you to have a good time, and he knows, Eve, that if you eat of the fruit of that tree, that you will be just like God. You will know good from evil." See how subtle he is. He mixes just enough truth with it to make it believable. They should know good from evil all right. They were living in the middle of God's good and love and by eating the fruit they would know evil by experience.

But Satan outright lied when he said that she would be like God. This is the way he works. He plants thoughts, he denies the word of God, he moves in with just enough truth to get his hideous lies accepted.

REECE GRAY

DOVE

BILL LANDERS

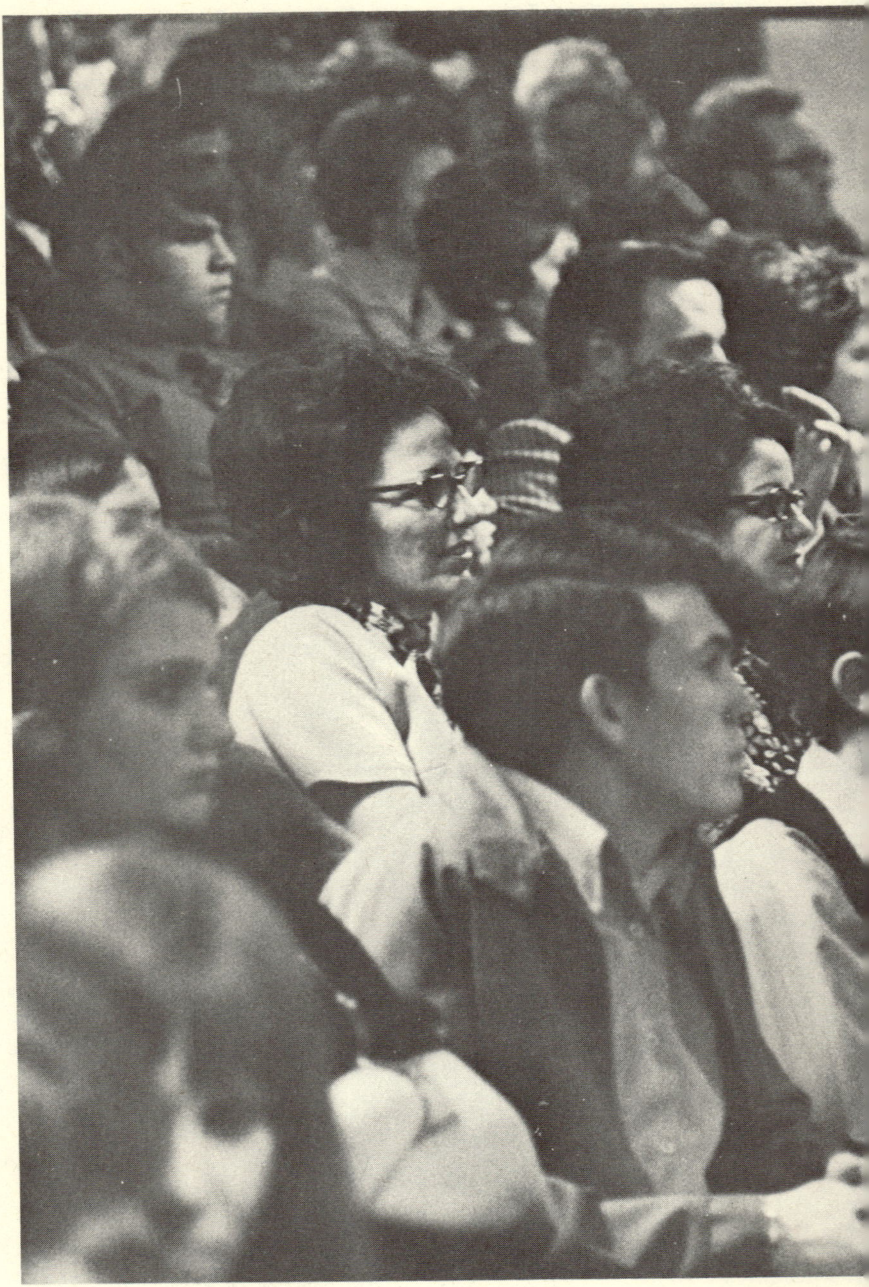

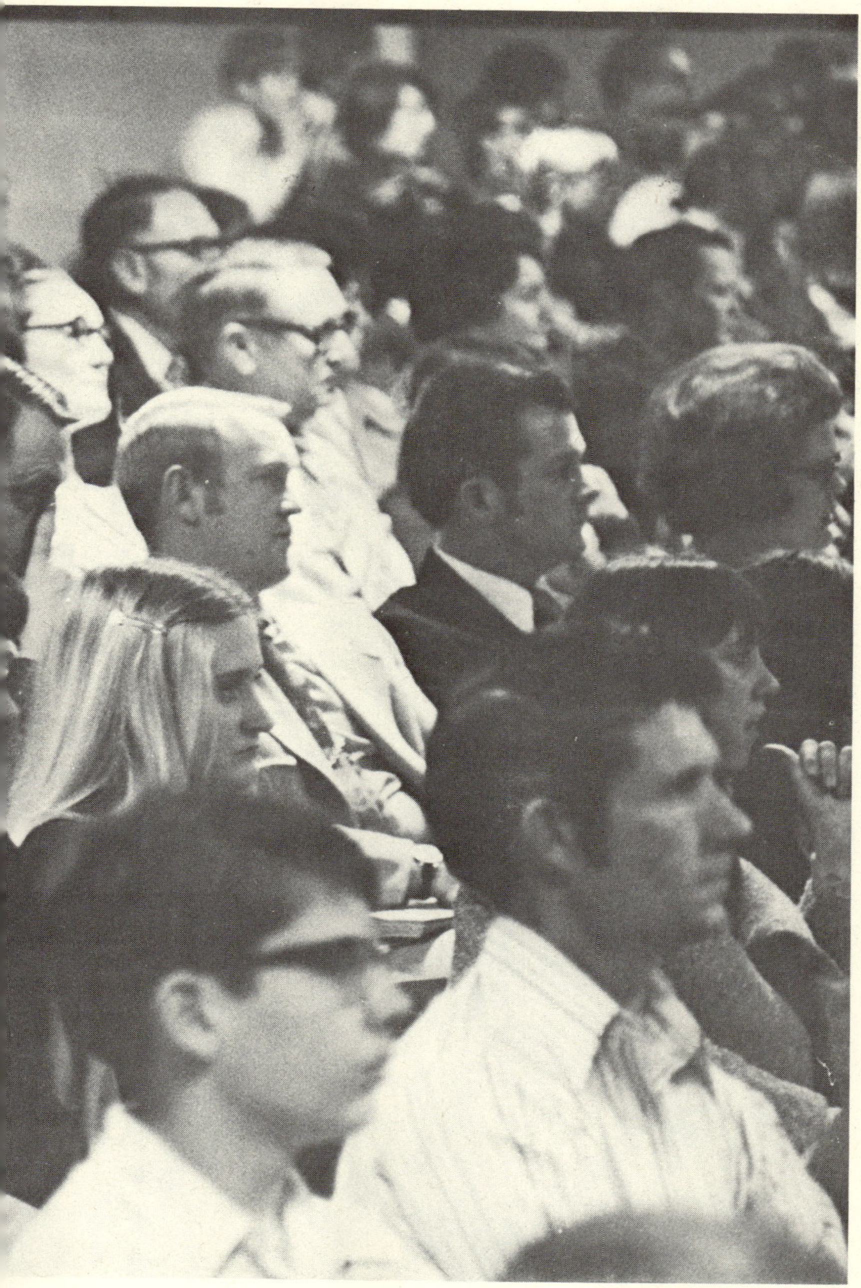

MARY MAULDIN

DAVE SMITH

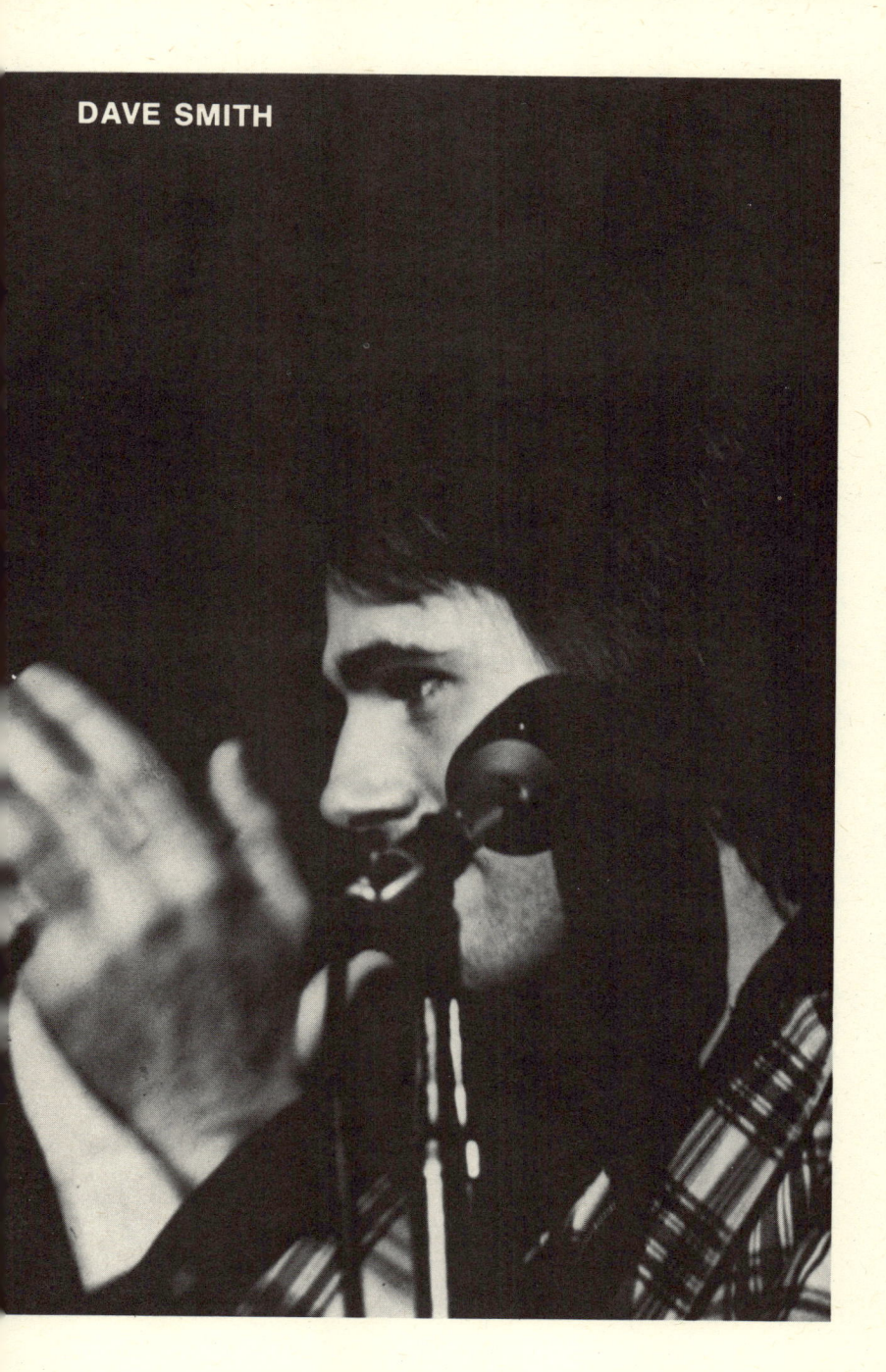

SONNY LALLERSTEDT

RANDY BUGG

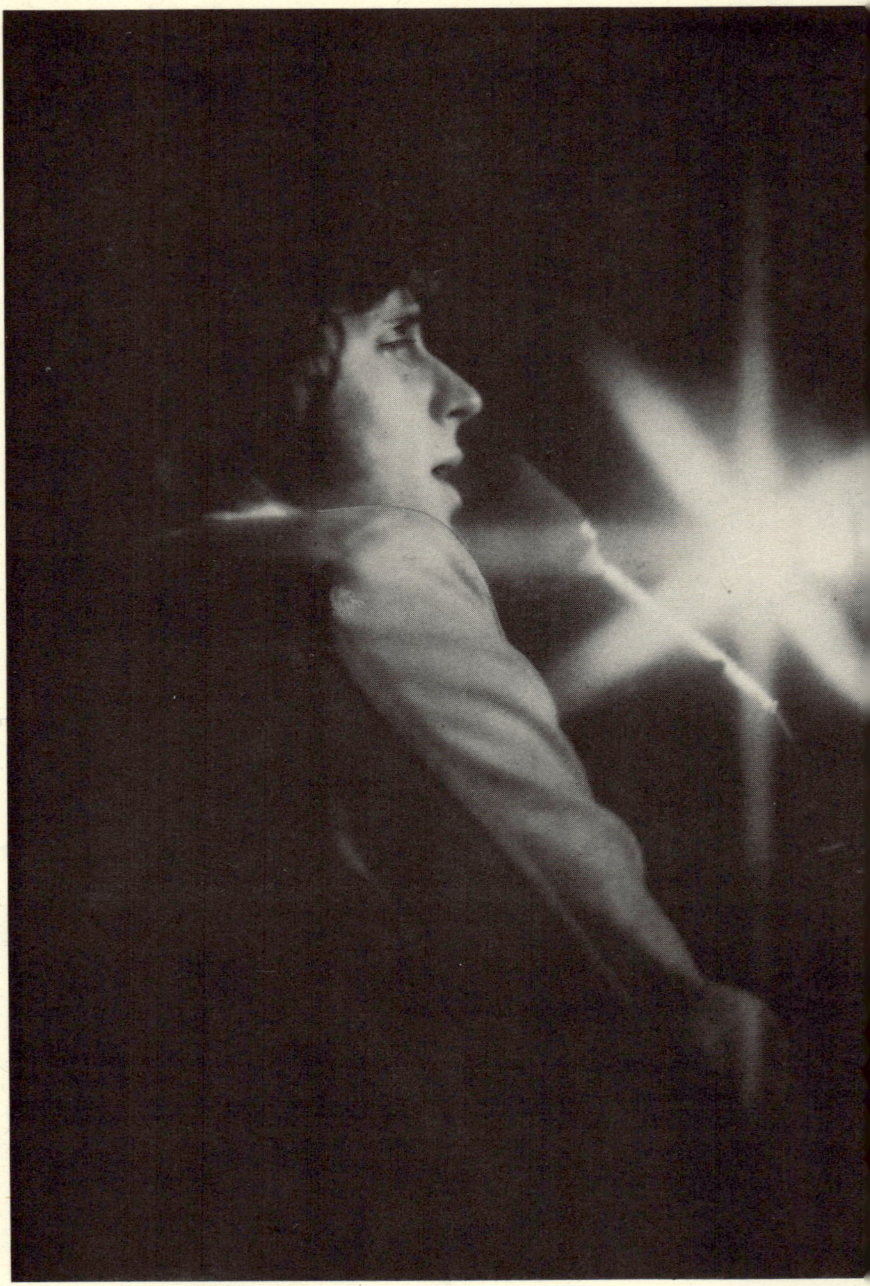

Now Eve was faced with a decision. Who would she believe, God or the serpent? By the looks of the outcome, Eve chose to believe God was really the liar and the serpent or Satan was actually telling the truth. In Verse 6, the Scripture says when the woman saw that the tree was good and that it was pleasant to the eyes, and when she thought about it making her wise, she took it. Satan called on his old ally of lust. He had her exactly where he wanted her. And then moved in for the kill. He said to take it, and she did.

When you really think about this temptation in the Garden, you realize that Eve knew the command of God. She knew God's will. She had been fellowshipping with him day by day, everyday of her life. Her downfall came when she allowed Satan to start substituting logic for God's word. The tree wasn't any different. It did look good. But God said, *do not eat it!* That should have settled the matter, but it didn't. She listened to Satan, and he talked her into open rebellion against God. And—watch this—as soon as she ate, things began to happen.

Someplace hanging around the Garden was Adam. In fact, when you read Genesis 3:6, you realize that he may have been right there with her and listened to the entire conversation with the serpent. But be that as it may, immediately after she had eaten of the tree, he did too. He chose to go with the woman and do what she had done instead of following God's command. Adam simply gave in without a fight, without lifting a finger. Satan had finished what he had wanted to accomplish. Since God had given Adam ownership of this world, when Adam chose against God and chose to follow Satan, Satan became the prince of the world, as Jesus called him in the Scriptures.

It was done. Man had fallen, and it is Satan's goal to this day to get every person in the world to choose to rebel against God and go with him.

At first glimpse, it really does not make sense. Why in the world would God allow someone to come into the middle of his created paradise and tear all hell *into* everything. Where did this guy come from? Who is he? Did God, who created everything in this world, create a character like this? Did God create Satan who seemingly only had the purpose to destroy the rest of God's creation?

Well, the Bible is very plain, and if you expect to get victory in this world—not only in the realm of sex, but in any other temptation that you are going to face day to day—there are some basic things you are going to have to know about Satan and how he works.

Who is this guy? We now know him as Satan or the devil, but when God created him he was known by the name of Lucifer, which means "the brilliant one" or "the shining one." And he was quite a different personality.

In fact, the Bible says, in Ezekiel 28:12, that he was "the perfection of wisdom and beauty" (The Living Bible). He was God's most beautiful created being. Remember, God did not create Satan—the Satan we know today—God created Lucifer. And God created him in total perfection. The Scripture says in Ezekiel 28:15: "You were perfect in your ways from the day you were created until iniquity was found in you."

What a fantastic beginning. Lucifer was, first of all, the wisest of all of God's created beings and the most powerful. God had established him as an administrator of the affairs of the angelic kingdom.

He occupied the highest position of all and had the greatest privilege of any one created being. He was able to enter into the very presence of God. In Ezekiel 28:13 the prophet says that Lucifer was the ultimate, beautiful work of God's creations. He says that every precious stone was his covering: the sardius, the topaz, the diamond, the beryl, the onyx, the jasper, the sapphire, the emerald, the carbuncle—all in beautiful settings of gold" (The Living Bible).

Think of it. Every possible color is found in these stones. But the amazing thing about these stones is that they have no light of their own. Their color only shows when light reflects from them. In the same way, Lucifer was made to have beauty only as God's light was reflected from him. Just as the moon reflects the light of the sun, Lucifer was to reflect the light and beauty of God.

Lucifer's job in God's creation was to be the head angel, reflect God's glory, and sing constant praises unto the Lord, because the Bible says in so many words that he was like a grand organ. He was God's music man. Lucifer constantly brought praises, honor, and glory to God.

It is hard for us to realize the strategic place and unbelievable power which God had given to Lucifer. How in the world, or maybe we should ask how in the heavens, could someone of such created beauty who is second in authority to the Godhead in heaven, how could someone of such magnificent greatness become as wicked and disobedient and deceitful and destructive as Lucifer? Watch closely, because in Lucifer's fall we can see that if someone of his great position could fall, how much easier it would be for man to fall in the same way. We read in Ezekiel 28:16-17 that Lucifer tried openly to rebel against God.

Lucifer became very proud and cocky. The Scripture says: "Your great wealth filled you with internal turmoil and you sinned . . . your heart was filled with pride because of your beauty; you corrupted your wisdom for the sake of your splendor." The fantastic wisdom and knowledge that God had given to Lucifer was distorted and perverted. Lucifer said in so many words, "I am so wise I ought to be God. Something as beautiful as me is being wasted by just being an angel. I should be worshipped." "I should not have to sit around and praise someone else." His pride and his vanity overwhelmed him. Lucifer was so filled with self that he wanted to own the glory, the praises, the honor that belonged only to God. In fact, he wanted to take over heaven. He wanted to rule the entire created existence, every area of this universe. He wanted to be free from all external authority. He declared his independence. He said in essence, I am going to be God. I am going to do what I want to do.

In Isaiah 14, five times we see Lucifer's pride as it just blows his mind wide open. First of all, he says, "I will ascend into heaven." The Bible says there are three categories of heaven. One is the one where airplanes fly around; the second is where the stars and the planet and far-removed galaxies are; and the third is where God lives. Now Lucifer worked in the third heaven, but he did not live there. You could say a desire for better housing was the first sin. Lucifer said, "I think I like this place so well, I think I will take over."

The second "I will" was when Lucifer said, "I will exhalt my throne above the stars and the angels of God." Now when God created the angelic realm, he had a structure

Meet Public Enemy Number One

of authority—hierarchy, as it would be. In the back of Lucifer's mind, he said, "I am going to pull off a coup and establish my own followers in the real positions of authority."

Thirdly, Lucifer said, "I will sit up on the Mount of the Congregation." No doubt about it, Lucifer was after everything God had.

Then Lucifer declared, "I will ascend above the heights of the clouds." Clouds usually mean glory. In other words, my glory is going to be greater than the glory of God.

The final "I will" was when Lucifer said, "I will be like the most High." In other words, Lucifer said, I am going to rule. I am going to possess this world, this universe, all of creation. If he could get where he could be judge, he could simply judge God out of God's position. He did not say, "I am going to be *un*like the most High." He was no dummy. He knew God had a good thing going. In fact, it was God's good thing he wanted to completely control. Some people think he wanted to be just the opposite of God, but in fact the opposite is true. He wanted to get his hands on everything God had. He wanted to rule. Lucifer wanted to be totally and completely independent of any authority outside of himself. Lucifer flat wanted to run things.

Lucifer's only sin—in fact, the only avenue of sin available to him—was to be independent from the authority of God. He couldn't go out and get drunk. He couldn't do some trivial little sin that we would think of. He had almost all the authority in heaven. All he was commanded to do was to obey God. Disobedience was the only sin available to him.

Now what generated such an insane, inconceivable, lust for power? One word. PRIDE.

Now, let's be logical. You might not be the most brilliant person in the world, but it only makes sense that a created being like Lucifer, as magnificent as he was, could never have gotten away with open rebellion against almighty God. He would have been out of his head even to have tried. As Dr. L. S. Chafer would say, it was "angelic insanity." The Scriptures say his mind was clouded over with pride. In other words, pride took all his rationality away. And, my friend, any time you sin, you are being just as stupid. You know you will never get away with it, but Satan uses your pride to blind you. Satan tells you that you can get away with it. No one will know, Satan says. But God records every event of history.

You say, "I am going to be God, I am going to do what I want to do, live the way I want to live, have sex if I want to, and there is no one big enough to tell me I can't." That, in so many words, is "HUMAN INSANITY."

You may say, if God knew that Lucifer and eventually man was going to rebel, why in the world did he give him the right to rebel?

The answer is very simple. God wants your love. He could have programed us like robots to have our obedience, our worship, our honor, our respect, but never our love. Love is something we must voluntarily give. Lucifer, as well as man, has chosen to give his love to himself. That's sin. That's the rebellion that turned Lucifer into Satan.

Satan was created not by God, but by rebellion against God.

Meet Public Enemy Number One

Now that Satan has been laid off of his job in heaven, he has taken up a new line of work on earth. His goal is to sell the philosophy of rebellion to every single person who lives—and he is doing magnificently well. In fact, he may be named any day now as the "most outstanding salesman" of our generation.

When Satan sold his first false philosophy policy to Adam and Eve, he really made a haul. In return for a piece of fruit, Adam surrendered unto Satan his title as the Prince of the World. If you think the Indians got rooked by selling all of Manhattan Island for a few beads, Adam traded the entire world for a piece of fruit. And God is bound because of his justice to honor the transaction until he brings this world to an end, and takes control himself—which he has every right to do, since Jesus defeated Satan at the cross. Just as Satan outsmarted Adam and Eve, Jesus outsmarted Satan at the cross, and, therefore, he was also able to serve Satan his eventual eviction notice.

But for right now, Satan is very much involved in things. And you are at the very center of his destructive strategy. Just as he moved in the Garden of Eden—by suggestion, lust, and lies—in the very same way he will try to move into your life and get you to commit the same sin he has committed, that sin of rebellion against God. And if you do, the same eternal punishment of hell will also be your punishment.

It really boggles your mind to realize that Satan was able to walk right into the middle of Eden and cause God's first created man to rebel, especially since Adam and Eve enjoyed daily fellowship and conversation with the Creator, God. It causes you to realize how extremely powerful Satan really is. And if a person today ever expects to get victory over Satan and not to succumb to his lusts and lies to drive us away from God's plan and laws for our lives, we must know how he works. Without that knowledge, we have "had it."

There are some basic things you need to know:

1. Satan is *not* all-powerful. He *can* be defeated.

2. He is *not* omnipresent (everywhere at once), even though he controls a world-wide demonic army which is in constant war against the mind of man. You see, one-third of the angels gave allegiance to Satan when Satan rebelled. And they have come to this world and now are his loyal servants, doing anything he desires. The Scripture calls these fallen angels demons. And even though Satan cannot be hassling everyone in the world at once, his demons can. What an army!

3. He is an imitator. He imitates the things of God. Why? Because God's plans for controlling the world are perfect, and it is those plans that Satan wants to control. He knows a good thing when he sees it. His real desire is to imitate or take the place of God.

4. He is the father of all lies. Jesus told us that. It has been true since he lied to himself in heaven about being able to overthrow God. He will try to lie to you about sex and about any other law of God he can get you to disobey.

5. He hates God's authority. That is why he wants you to rebel against God, against his laws for sex and every single area of your life.

6. He is like a roaring lion, seeking whom he may devour (1 Pet. 5:8). Now, if you know anything about lions

Meet Public Enemy Number One

you know that they roar only after they have made their kill. Today Satan has much to roar about! But he is making all his kills by bluffing. Because of the cross, he's a lion without teeth. If he defeats you, it will be because you just give in and surrender to his roar, his bluff.

7. He is our adversary. When you have wanted to do what is right but constantly thought about doing what is wrong in the eyesight of God, that temptation comes from our adversary who is longing to destroy you, Satan.

8. He wants like crazy to control your thoughts, because then he can control your actions.

9. He hates the Bible and would love to destroy it, mainly because it shows him to be the crook that he is, and it shows man how to know Jesus and have perfect fellowship with God.

10. He hates Jesus not only since he is the One who defeated him at the cross, but also because Jesus will one day judge Satan and all those who follow him to everlasting hell.

11. He does not want man to realize that Jesus has the power to free him from Satan's power; because if man ever realized that, Satan's constant lying and deception of man would come to a quick end.

12. As powerful as he is, there are still only a few ways in which Satan can attack. The Bible says, in fact, there are just three. First of all, the *lust of the flesh.* This is where he attacks many people with sex and drugs and alcohol—the physical thrill behind sin. Satan uses this to draw us away from God. Then the Bible says he will attack us by getting us to become *selfish.* We will quit loving other people. We want everything for ourselves. We be-

come jealous. We like to put someone down. We want to be number one, like Satan when he was kicked out of heaven. And then his big attack comes through *pride* (Prov. 16:8; Col. 2:15). Remember it was pride that caused Satan to rebel against God, and Satan uses our pride to get us where we want to run our own lives, call our own shots. God can go hang. We become very self-sufficient and confident. We begin to trust our own power. When we do, we refuse to acknowledge God as the ultimate authority. Since we're trusting in our own inflated ability, instead of God's power, we're perfect game for Satan. The only power greater than his is God's.

13. Satan places the thought of rebellion (temptation) in your mind. Then he tries to get you to let it stay there long enough to grow into the real desire of your life so he can take those desires and turn them into disobedience to God. This is especially true with sex. He gets you to look at pornographic books, illicit movies, some "braless chick." He places that thought in your mind. Then every time you turn around for the next few days, he constantly places that thought in your mind, places that thought in your mind, places that thought in your mind. And when you don't do anything about that thought, you allow Satan to start controling your mind to the place that that thought becomes the real desire of your heart. Then you've almost *got* to have sex. It becomes almost an unquenchable desire until you have fulfilled that lust which began simply as a thought in your mind from Satan. You see, once you start to love the temptation that Satan places in your mind, the very next thing for you to do is to go ahead and do what that temptation of Satan is wanting you to do.

14. Satan is a perverter of the things of God. One giant example is the way he has tried totally to rearrange and destroy the sexual laws of God. He has destroyed these things for his own destructive ends (Rom. 1:25). A perfect example is the first chapter of Romans. This Scripture says that men, instead of believing what they know to be true, deliberately chose to believe lies, just as Eve in the Garden chose to believe Satan over God. That's Satan. In Verses 26-27, we see that when they believed the lies, they turned against God's laws for sex and committed open homosexuality. Satan tries to destroy any gift God has, from sex to salvation.

15. Satan tries to get us to believe that if we follow Jesus and his rules for life, we will really miss out on the fun of life. The exact opposite is true.

16. Dr. James Mahoney says in his fantastic new book, *Journey Into Fullness* that Satan attacks us in two distinct ways. First of all, by *oppression*. In other words, he flat out attacks us. He tries to depress us, to get us to yield to temptation. And then he comes to us through suggestion, like he did with Eve. He suggested something to her that was against the will of God. He did not force her. He simply planted the suggestion and she fell for it.

17. Satan does not have all authority. Remember, Jesus is Lord. That means that Jesus is BOSS!

18. Satan especially wants us not to think he is real. That way, he can have the freedom to bomb us out without even being noticed.

But why? The question must be asked. Why would Satan be so interested in destroying man and getting him to go against God for his life? Why? Because Satan wants to produce his own sin in our lives. You see, when Satan rebelled against God and blew his plans to take over God's position, he was kicked out of heaven, and there was no way for him to lead another coup against God. He had been banished for eternity. After he got one-third of the angels to rebel and go with him, then God sealed the will of the rest of the angels so Satan could never hassel them any more. Then when God created man, Satan saw his next opportunity to win the victory over God. Man had been placed on earth as God's administrator, so Satan had an opportunity, if not to win permanently from God, at least to destroy his plan. Satan knows of God's love for man. And the reason he hates man so much is because of Jesus' great love for man.

At this moment, as you are reading this book, your mind is the battlefield on which spiritual warfare is now taking place; and amazingly, as God and Satan vie for your love and obedience, the one who has the right to determine the outcome of the battle is you. Just as God will not force you to do his will, Satan *cannot* force you. The ultimate decision is yours!

5

If You Love Me, Prove It!

A girl in Arkansas was mature for her age. Though she was only fifteen, she had matured physically and emotionally. She became infatuated with a boy. They started going steady. He was a junior in high school. Soon they were finding opportunities to park. The affection grew. When she finally discussed this with her minister, she openly admitted that she had been having sexual relations with the boy at least twice a week for several months. But they were too young to get married. Besides, how would they finish school?

When the family doctor was consulted, he gave this counsel: "She has been having intercourse now for several months. You may succeed in getting her to break up with this boy, but before long, she will have the same problem with another boy. Having tasted the intimacies of sex, she will not be able to put it out of her mind. If she starts going with someone else, she will soon be sleeping with him. Once a girl begins to have intercourse frequently she usually cannot stop. It might be better to let her marry this boy than to let her develop a reputation of sleeping with every boy she dates."

The marriage consent was given. They were both college material, but both dropped out of school. Now, the boy works as a laborer, wondering what he could have become if he had not met her. She is raising a family on a meager income, asking in her heart if he really loves her, or ever loved her, or if he just got trapped and then couldn't get out of it. No wonder someone said that the greatest tragedies of all are the things that might have been.

This boy and girl had an experience similar and common to many. There is one thing you can say for the devil. He has no new tricks. He uses the same sex tricks on everyone. The story, the methods, the scenes are all the same.

Only the names have been changed to protect the guilty. One of the best examples of a sex-destructed life is the young long-haired teen-ager, Samson. Samson had everything. He was strong, good-looking; when he walked into a room, the girls went ape. They wanted to get their fingers into Samson's hair (most of them did; that was what was wrong). He looked like a Greek god, Mr. America, and Tom Jones all rolled into one.

One day, Samson got into a fight with some local crooks. Man, he really got mad, so he picked up the jawbone of a donkey (a dead one) and wiped out a thousand people on the spot. Superman never did anything like that.

Another time he was having a little argument with some people in a village. So he went out and caught several foxes, set their tails on fire, ran them through the village, and burned it to the ground. Samson made James Bond look like Mickey Mouse. He was God's super agent; the enemy was scared to death of him. He was a spiritual giant, God's number one guy. God loved him, God used him, God was with him. Then Samson began to play around with sex. He would fight for God one morning, then go out with the local chicks in the evening. He stopped keeping God in the center of his life. He stopped living really to serve the Lord and began to serve his own appetite of lust and pleasure. Then it happened. Satan brought in the most beautiful girl, named Delilah. She was the most gorgeous creature Samson had ever seen. The devil is no dummy. He will always make sex look good. He wraps it in a gold box with a big red bow on it. He is an expert at packaging and marketing. He always makes a mistake look like something you can't do without, and that is what he did to Samson.

Delilah set out immediately to bring this giant of a man down. She got his attention, wrapped him in her charm, and immediately set out to destroy him.

She said, "If you love me, Samson, tell me the secret of your strength." Nothing new about that line, is there? You have heard it plenty of times: "If you really love me, you will let me do what I want to." Think how ridiculous that is. The only thing that line proves is the selfishness of the person who uses it. He is really saying to you, "Let me prove how selfish I can be by using your body."

Recently, someone said in *Christianity Today* that a worker in the orange groves of Florida occasionally will take out a knife and cut away the top of an orange. He then takes it in his hands, sucks and squeezes until the pulp is dry, and then throws what is left on the ground. "I just love oranges," he says. What he really means is, "oranges do something for me." He doesn't really love them; he uses them. He wants to get what he can from them.

How can some women be so blind? How can a woman give a man her body simply because he says the magic words "I love you"? What he really means is, "You turn me on. I want to take what I can get from you." That's not love. It's selfishness. Genuine love involves respect, a respect that can be tested with the question, "Does he (or she) look at me as a person, or as a thing?"

Meanwhile, back at the bedroom, we find that Delilah has coaxed Samson into saying he will tell her the secret of his strength. "If you bind me with seven undried stalks of grain, that is the secret of my strength." So she took seven undried stalks of grain and tied him up with them. Then she called in the enemy soldiers. But Samson knew some tricks, too. He fooled her. He broke the stalks in an instant and killed everyone in the room. Then Delilah came up with a line which has been used for centuries: "If you don't do what I want to do, I just won't date you anymore." Actually, you ought to thank God when someone tells you that. If that is all he dates you for, you're lucky he won't be around to bother you again.

In Weatherford, Texas, about 5:30 one evening, I was in a restaurant eating a meal right before our evening service. A young lady came over to our table. She was young, about seventeen. She had recognized me and came over and said, "Richard, I must talk with you. Could I take a few moments of your time?" After she was seated, tears almost instantly came to her face. It was very evident that the things that were bothering her had hurt her very deeply.

If You Love Me, Prove It! 77

Through the tears she began to tell me she had had an affair with a young soldier from a nearby military base. "When I first met the boy," she said, "he seemed like a real sharp person. We really had a good time together. After we had been out together four or five times, he told me he loved me and that he knew I was the only girl for him, the one he wanted to marry and spend his life with. Then he started saying, 'If you really love me, prove it.' I really did love him," she said, "and I wanted like crazy to keep him, so I proved it, and I kept on proving it every night we went out. Then about a week before he was to be transferred to another base, he told me it was all over. I just couldn't understand what had happened. But then the pieces began to fall into place, horribly into place. He was married and he had a daughter and he didn't love me." I wish I could describe the deep hurt and bitterness that was in her face.

Back in the bedroom again, Samson had told Delilah that the secret of his strength was being tied up with new ropes. Again she tied him up, and again Samson broke loose. But Delilah was literally as "patient as the devil." (In fact, if the devil has any virtues, that is one of them. He is very patient. He is in no hurry to destroy your life. He takes his time, and when you think you have him whipped, there he is back again.)

A girl may think that if she really lays down the rules on a date, the next time she goes out with a boy he will respect her convictions. That seldom happens. There is only one exception to that. That is when the boy makes a commitment of his life to Jesus between the first date and the second date.

So Delilah was not discouraged. In fact, she was now even more determined than ever to destroy her superman. Samson fooled her one more time by telling her to tie up seven locks of his hair. Notice how he kept getting closer and closer to the real secret of his strength. That is how the devil always works. He begins slowly and then he works up to his final point. He doesn't go right up and slug you in the mouth. Instead, he begins slowly. He finds that weakest point—that weak area in which he can enter and tempt you, that area which he can get to again, slowly like a cancer that begins to eat away at you until he can finally destroy your life.

The Arabs have a good story about a camel. One winter day the mill owner was sleeping in his house and is awakened by a noise. Looking up, he saw that a camel had stuck his nose through the door. "It is very cold out here," said the camel. "Please let me warm my nose a little." Finally, the miller said, "All right, but just your nose."

A little later, the camel asked permission to put his forehead in. It was given. After another thirty minutes, he wanted to put his neck in. Little by little, he kept crowding in until finally his whole body was in the miller's house. Another hour passed. Then the camel began to walk around the room, knocking things over and doing just as he pleased. The miller was so irritated by this that he told the camel to leave.

"If you do not like the room, you can leave it whenever you wish," replied the camel. "As for myself, I am very comfortable and mean to stay where I am."

The devil is very careful. He starts slowly, saying, "Oh, you can stop whenever you want; you'll never go all the

If You Love Me, Prove It!

way." That is exactly what he wants you to think. He wants you to take your time, just long enough to give him a hold. There are a lot of things that get into your life just like that, a little at a time. But once inside, they keep gaining power until they eventually become the master of your soul. The devil starts with something like shabby literature and shabby movies to turn your mind on to the thrill of sexual stimulation. Soon, you can't get it off your mind. After all, it doesn't really hurt anything to play with sexual ideas. Sex is a fun toy. Then Friday night comes. It starts with just a kiss, and before you know it you have rationalized yourself into the petting stage, and you go all the way.

That is exactly what happened to Samson. All that he could have been—God's chosen MAN. Delilah stuck with him long enough to finally get him to tell her the secret of his strength. That superman of God fell to the temptation and told her. She put Samson to sleep on the couch and got the local barber to come in and shave his head. Then she went and got a bunch of Philistine soldiers. They came into the room and got all around the couch. Delilah leaned over and woke Samson up. As soon as he got up and saw the enemy, he roared up off that couch and said, "Step aside, Delilah, I am going to whip me some Philistines." But the Bible says he didn't know that the Lord had departed from him. They jumped on him, wrestled him to the ground, tied him up, got hot coals from the fire, and put his eyes out. Then they tied him up like an animal, took him down to the enemy mill, and made him take the place of an ox going 'round and 'round grinding the grain in the mill.

Now, brother, he was God's chosen man with all the potential in the world. He could have been one of the greatest men that ever lived, another Moses, another Abraham, yet he blew it in a moment.

That happens to a lot of the young men and women. They push a great life ten miles out of reach, then blow it all with one careless moment.

David is another example of the ideal man. He was a man after God's own heart. But when he took his eyes off God and put them on a woman, he changed from the chosen, the anointed of God, to a man who stooped to first-degree murder in order to fulfill his lust. Satan literally wiped David out. It was not just a drive for sex with a certain person; his entire personality was changed.

You see David in the Scriptures before his sin with Bathsheba when he was so concerned for his troops, how he loved his soldiers. You see how when some of his soldiers had had their hair shaved by the enemy, David told them that they did not have to come home until it grew out some so no one would embarrass them. Yet, in the next chapter, David's entire personality changed. WHY?

Brother, Satan got hold of his mind. David did not expect him to show up right under his nose. He did not expect to meet with temptation, and he did not know how subtly the devil worked. But when his eyes saw a beautiful naked woman taking a bath, he did something which he would never have thought of going to a prostitute for. Do not forget that. The worst temptation is never far away. The things that make us fall are usually right in front or very close to us.

If You Love Me, Prove It!

In the first Psalm David recorded (even though he did not know it at the time) the steps of his own failure of sin in the area of sex: "Blessed is the man that walketh not in the counsel of the ungodly, nor standeth in the way of sinners, nor sitteth in the seat of the scornful." He caught a glimpse at Bathsheba naked, and when he did, he stopped and stood and began to lust. Now, David probably was unable to miss seeing Bathsheba; but just seeing her was not the sin. The sin took place when he stood and waited and opened up his mind and, as the Bible says, "nor sitteth in the seat of the scornful." In other words, David walked by sin, stood and looked at it, and finally sat down to enjoy it. You see how subtly Satan works.

A young man I know was a devoted Christian. How could he possibly go wrong? But he did. The part-time secretary for his office was a beautiful, vivacious girl who had married an older man. She was not happy with him. The young man was like David—good-looking, strong, a man of great personal force. One day in the office, it happened. Without a word, it happened. The accumulated effect of the mini-skirt, the feeling of the moment, a failure to see that you must always be alert to temptation, and it happened. Time went by, and it happened again. Now he looked forward to it. It became a part of his life. Why? He had convinced himself that a small flirtation was an innocent matter. But it ended up not so innocent. He gained some free sex and a few thrills, but, like David, he lost his job, his wife, his family, and his future.

A girl in Oklahoma told me that God just wasn't helping her in the area of sex. When she said that, I knew something wasn't right. When I quizzed her further, the truth came to light. She told me that God had been telling her that she should not attend certain kinds of movies because she got sexually aroused. Yet she kept going to them. And she paid no attention to God's directions about whom she dated. She put herself right in the middle of the devil's trap and then yelled, "Help, God!" That is like standing at the edge of a cliff and saying, "Come on devil, push."

Remember that it is the little decisions which produce the big troubles. Very few boys make conscious decisions to go out and get someone to have intercourse with them. Very few girls make conscious plans before going to the drive-in to invite their boyfriends to make love to them. It is the little decisions to park, to see a sexually arousing show, to tell a sexy joke, to let the petting start—there is where the big decision is made. You still make the decision. When you put the clothes on and that dress is too short, you know in your mind what you want that dress to do. When you go braless on your date, don't let Satan kid you into saying it is just because it is more comfortable. You know what is going to happen.

The Bible says the wayward sinner is as a sheep. Why? Because sheep don't run away. They just nibble themselves lost. When a sheep starts to eat, the green grass draws him further and further away until he finally is lost. He just nibbles himself lost. That is the way we get ourselves lost sexually. We nibble ourselves lost.

Some of you women ought to do your "sisters" and yourselves a favor by not letting a man get away with taking sex from you like candy from a baby. He is likely to expect more of the same from the next woman. True liberation means that you have just as much right to say no as to say yes. Now, let's be honest. Rarely is a man or a woman so swept along with passion that he does not realize what he is doing until it is all over. There is always a point at which a person will realize that if he goes any further he is going to go all the way. By not stopping, a boy or girl carries out a conscious decision. Passion is very real and exciting, but it is not mindless. Of course, if you have been smoking grass or drinking, you can blame your actions on that; but if you think about it, you really are fooling only yourself. You are the one who decides.

If you really want to avoid sex relations, you will watch who you date, what you wear, and where you go. You will call on God in the beginning when the devil is dishing out the smaller temptations, when you can completely avoid the bigger ones. The time to yell out is when you are sinking, not after you already have drowned.

David did not yell out, and he reaped what he sowed. Everything he wanted was at his fingertips. His dream to build the Temple vanished. His children turned on him and became his deepest sorrow. Even his favorite and beloved son rebelled against him in an open way and was gruesomely hanged when his long hair caught in a tree branch while he was fighting his father's troops. What Proverbs says about wine is also true of sex sins: "Don't let the sparkle deceive you, for in the end it bites likes a poisonous serpent, it stings like an adder" (Prov. 23:31-32).

I have met hundreds of modern-day Samsons and Davids all over America. One was a young woman who, like Samson and David, had everything. She was naturally beautiful, with olive skin and golden hair, intelligent, multi-talented. Every boy in school wanted to date her. She had her pick. She was in church every Sunday, but on Friday and Saturday nights, she began fulfilling her lust. One thing led to another—the kiss to the caress, the caress to petting, that to a habit, and a habit to intercourse. Today, the beautiful blond hair still is blond, but the face it surrounds is no longer a happy "live it up, take all you can get" face. Its beauty is gone. It has hardened to a mask of sorrow, loneliness, bitterness, and a sort of reticent despair. Judgment fell upon her just as it did upon Samson and David. She got what she wanted, but now she has to live with it. Now, after two illegitimate children and a marriage that ended in disloyalty and divorce, a once beautiful young woman has learned to live with a ruined life.

6

What's So Great About Being a Virgin?

A young couple came up to me one night on the Miami University campus in Ohio and in all seriousness asked this question: "What is so great about being a virgin?" Today this question needs to be answered very seriously. In our confused, sex-oriented socieity, most people have forgotten the values of keeping themselves untangled from sexual sins.

Wanting to be pure before marriage, as we have seen earlier in this book, is considered to be a joke to many; but there are some very definite physical as well as spiritual reasons to obey the commands of God to keep sex within the bounds of marriage.

For one thing, virgins (of both sexes) get to miss venereal disease. We used to think the diseases only involved sailors and soldiers and houses of prostitution. Perhaps they did once, but not now. Venereal disease is now at an all time high in America. As well as a lot of free new pleasure, the new freedom of the pill is bringing us a lot of free new pain.

Another piece of false information that we hear across the country is that the pill can prevent VD infection. In fact, it apparently adds an extra susceptibility factor. According to Dr. Walter Smartt of the Los Angeles County Health Department, "Women on the pill seem more liable to VD infections and complications."

The Government cut back on funds for VD programs at the very time that sexual promiscuity was increasing. Less money is now available for tracking down and treating persons infected with VD. Since the pill does not provide protection, VD has reached epidemic proportions in many regions of America.

Dr. William F. Brown, Chief of the Venereal Disease Branch of the Bureau of State Services of the Communicable Disease Center, Atlanta, Georgia, says that the number of cases of infectious syphilis among teen-agers has increased 232 percent since 1957 and 246 percent among young adults. He further states: "We estimate 100,000 cases of syphilis are diagnosed but go unreported each year." The rise of VD is unbelievable. Many strains are now developing that are immune to the modern medicine we thought was the answer. Gonorrhea can produce the most frightful suffering and lifelong invalidism in women. It still is the number one cause of lifelong blindness in the next generation. Dr. S. I. McMillen says in his book, *None of These Diseases:* "How tragic it is that hundreds of thousands of hopelessly blind people must pay the devil for the sins of their parents."

Dr. Brown goes on to say: "Syphilis is also the cause of many a baby's being born macerated and dead. If an infected baby lives, it may have various physical or mental deficiencies. Not only do these handicapped children have to pay a price during their lives, but their parents, as they look daily on their deformed or insane children, must pay dearly and bitterly with lifelong remorse."

And not all the destructive action is immediate. Twenty years may go by after the disease is contracted before it strikes down its victim with a dreaded or fatal complication. One late manifestation of syphilis, for example, is "paresis," an insanity caused by syphilis hitting the brain cells. This insanity can develop in a person at any time from five to thirty years after the infection originates.

Sylvanus M. Duvall, in his article, "Fiction and Facts About Sex," told of a girl who thought she was safe because she had sexual relations with only one boyfriend. She was extremely surprised and upset when her doctor told her she was infected. As Duvall reports, "A 'venereal tracer' revealed that the boy had consorted with only one other girl. This girl had had relations with five other men who in turn had been with nineteen women, some of them prostitutes. The girl who thought her relationship had been limited to one person had contact, through him, with at least ninety-two others.

But this could not be true of a girl or boy that you date! Don't kid yourself. Doctors report that this disease is just as prevalent among the middle- and upper-class kids as it is the down-and-outers. A prominent street address does not turn back germs. Germs just don't read the society page anymore. To make things worse, many varieties of VD are like incurable cancer. You don't get over them. You just live with them until you die with them.

A father was making homemade fudge with his children. Mother wasn't home. Everything worked out fine until they got to the place where the recipe said, "Beat, and pour out on a cookie sheet." But they must have done something wrong. When they tried to pour the mixture, it came out in big chunks. It was all crumbly. The little girl asked, "Can't we cook it over?" The family had to tell her that you can't cook fudge over again. There are a lot of things in life you can't do over again. They are like making fudge. When they are done, they are done for good. Venereal disease is like that. When it's done, it's done.

Some have the erroneous thought that VD can come from only females. But in many areas, 20 percent or more of the infections are transferred by homosexual practices. And since male homosexuals usually make more "contacts" than those involved in heterosexual promiscuous sex, the problem is exploding among them. It is next to impossible for VD to be transmitted by public toilets, dirty doorknobs, drinking cups, eating utensils, water, food, or the air. Even the possibility of transmission by handshaking is remote. A knowledge of the nature of the syphilis and gonorrhea organisms shows why. The organisms are very fragile outside the human body. Removed from human tissues, they die within seconds or within a few minutes at the most. These organisms which thrive at body temperature cannot survive great variations of temperature. And even with all of our advances in medical science, there is no known immunizing vaccine for either syphilis or gonorrhea.

Another thing virgins miss is premarital pregnancy. The Chicago *Tribune* declares: "Forty-five percent of all teenage brides are already pregnant on their wedding days." And other reliable sources estimate that one-half to three-fourths of the high school boys who marry are involved in premarital pregnancies, not to mention how many have had sex relations and just were not caught. More and more authorities are comparing the United States with Sweden in its upsurging immorality. It is reported that in Sweden only five percent of the girls and two percent of the young men go to the marriage altar with their purity intact.

Another thing virgins miss is abortion. Take a look at the statistics on abortions in this country. It is now an epidemic. One girl out of six who is now thirteen years old will become illegitimately pregnant before she is twenty. That is two and a half times the rate it was ten years ago. This increase is not among girls of lower classes. It is mostly among the "nice" girls in the upper and middle classes.

Even though abortion has been legalized and many competent doctors now perform them safely, there are still the effects of abortion on the mind. One Christian psychiatrist friend of mine told me, "It is hard to imagine the severe emotional damages which occur with most abortions. Many times the girl who has to go to an abortionist grows to hate the man she loved so passionately. Her resentment at the humiliation of abortion seeks an outlet and usually destroys their love affair. Few girls ever marry the boys from whom they had aborted babies. Many girls are so hurt by their experience that they develop a hatred for all sexual relations. Their future sexual happiness in marriage is self-destructed before it starts."

If you are asking your girl, "Why shouldn't we go all the way before marriage?" there is a definite answer: because it is wrong; it is a sin. But even beyond that, maybe you should ask yourself: "Do I really love this girl?" Let's be honest. If you do love her, then you won't use her sex for your own selfishness to the point of endangering her future health and happiness.

The only way you can really prove your love for a girl is to keep her a virgin until you marry. Sexual purity is an expression of love, of loving enough not to want to hurt. So instead of asking, "Do *you* love *me* enough to do it?" the real question is, "Do *I* love *you* enough not to do it?"

Another thing virgins miss is a lot of frustration. There is much talk today about how hard it is to want sex and not get it until you are old enough to get married. But that frustration is nothing compared to the frustration which comes to people who practice this "free sex" they think they need.

Sex is such an emotion that when aroused without love it easily develops into hate. Often young people feel only contempt for each other later, because both know the other was "easy." Why make the very thing with which God has chosen to make man and woman complete, to make the two into one, why make it a plague? In your marriage it can be a fantastic adventure which the two of you can discover together for the very first time.

One prime reason sex outside marriage often leads to resentment and hatred is its destructive effect on self-respect—one of our most prized possessions. Virtue, on the other hand, increases self-respect. Dr. Francis Braceland, former President of the American Psychiatric Association and the editor of *The American Journal of Psychiatry,* reports that "pre-marital sex relations resulting from our so-called 'new morality' have significantly increased the

What's So Great About Being a Virgin?

number of young people in our mental hospitals." Over half of the hospital beds in America are filled with mental patients. And leading psychologists tell us that many of these cases come from sin leading to severe guilt complexes. A good example to substantiate this is Sweden, mentioned earlier for its sexual laxity. Sweden has one of the highest percentages of teenage suicide of any country in the world.

You say, "If I don't experience sex before marriage, how will I know if my future wife or husband and I are sexually compatible?" If God is God, he is certainly going to give you the perfect mate to complete you in every area, if you are in his will.

If you seek God's will instead of fulfilling your own lust, then he will give you his chosen one for you. It is amazing to me that all those people who say God has no perfect will and no perfect mate for you are the very ones who have had three or four marriages and are still not happy, who still try to improve on perfection.

God made you to begin with, and he knows better than you what it takes to fulfill you. So when you seek God's will to find that certain one, there is no need for comparison, no need for checking down the list—"Who can love the best," etc. Ridiculous! That is why it is so important not to park and share your body with everyone or anyone. When you find that special someone that God has chosen just for you, you'll wish you'd never even held hands with anybody else!

A Christian psychologist, Dr. Henry Brandt, tells the story of a lovely, intelligent young lady who made an appointment to see him. She was unhappy and miserable.

During college days Ann met Bill, a handsome man. He was intelligent and had cast off the "shackles" of "foolish rules about sex." Ann was inspired by this intellectual modern approach.

As they began to experience the pleasures of heavy petting, the usual began to happen. There was a growing desire for intimacy. This led to sexual relations. "After all, what is wrong with this?" they asked.

"Nothing, it's great," they answered each other, "so long as we both agree that there is no obligation involved."

But then some new shackles started forming. Ann lost interest in other men and wanted to be only with Bill. But he didn't see it that way. After all, they had an agreement. Ann hadn't bargained for the feelings that many times come with sexual life. Why couldn't she keep sex on a purely impersonal basis? She began to hate herself for her inability to be detached and her inability to shake off her deep love for Bill.

Then she started being jealous of him. She became bitter. It was impossible to study. She was irritable with her roommate, quarreled with Bill, and they separated. She was lonely, miserable, disappointed, angry, and, most of all, disgusted with herself.

"How can something so wonderful turn out so horrible?" she asked her counselor. She is not the first person to ask that question. She misjudged her human makeup. She could unhook from her moral code with her mind, but she couldn't unhook from her moral sexual emotions.

The story gets worse. In her miserable condition, her intelligence and judgment were short-circuited by her bitterness and emotion. She began to use her beauty and charms to entice other men. After she had them, she dropped them. She didn't realize it, but she was getting even with Bill. She ended up marrying someone with whom she had little in common. Ann and her husband quarreled constantly. She was at odds with her family and everyone. Now the thought of sexual relations nauseated her.

Satan. He is so clever. Believe his lie and he's got you where he wants you. Then he can move in for the kill.

It is staggering to see how high the divorce rate is in marriages of people who have experienced premarital sex. With almost every young couple I have ever counseled concerning their marriages (and psychologists report the same), I have found the problem to be mistrust. And many times both parties are being faithful. But because they did not keep themselves pure *before* marriage, they don't know if they can trust each other's purity *inside* of marriage.

This is the age of "pop" sex. Advertising, movies, and books tell us that sex can be disengaged from the other parts of our life. It is a toy to enjoy. That is the oversimplification of the century! You can't isolate sex from your other emotions. It is glued to you. Many people, even though they claim to be open-minded and enlightened, carry with them all their lives a hurt in their personalities that they can never get over.

But worst of all, the sexually promiscuous men and women often loose (and make those around them loose) the greatest experience in life—the deep love of one person. So, whenever you hear a person brag about his conquests, you can figure he is really putting up a sign in big bold letters, "Look how selfish I am. I want a lot of different people to love me, stimulate me, and make me feel good, but I am not willing to put myself on the line for any one person." The bragger is not really telling you that he is a great lover. He is telling you that he is a "non-lover."

Sex alone is not love. A preoccupation with sex, whether it is overpreoccupation, like we have today, or preoccupation with avoiding it, like many people had in the Victorian age, it's always a sign that people are in trouble. It always means that they are starved for love. They find themselves incapable of genuine love, so they try its closest substitute, which is sex.

Everything you do in life, you pay for. If you choose the narrow, straight gate of sexual purity, you certainly have to pay for it—with self-restraint and the determination to keep youself pure even at the risk of being put down and belittled. If you choose the wide gate of sexual promiscuity, you pay for that too. The difference between the two is when you pay for them, how long you pay, and the severity of the payment. If you choose sexual purity, you pay in advance. If you choose sexual sin, you pay for it later, after you get it—sometimes a long time after you get it—but you may pay for it the rest of your life, and often it can cost you your whole future happiness. So pay your nickel and take your choice. But don't be deceived. Either way, you have to pay.

7

Let Him Put It All Together

A boy came to me and said, "I don't know what's the matter with me. I try hard to be a Christian, but I always fail."

"What do you mean, you fail?" I asked him.

"It's the sex bit," he said. "I've always heard that sex outside of marriage is wrong. So I think to myself, 'I will avoid this like the plague.' Well, several months ago I was at a drive-in with this girl. We were going great, having a great time. The Bible doesn't say kissing is wrong, does it?" he asked. "After a few minutes of this, she whispered, 'If you love me, prove it.' Then she went ape! I thought the man was supposed to be the aggressor. Not with this chick. Afterwards I felt terrible. I thought a lot about it the next day and decided I wouldn't do it again. I was scared to death. What if she got pregnant? And I'm only a sophomore, so I decided that was all for me. But then the next week we went out again. She did the same thing again. I told her that I would like to, but that she might become pregnant. You know what she said? 'Oh, no. I'm on the pills. I do it all the time. Come on, don't be a chicken. If you love me . . .' Preacher, what do you do with a situation like that?"

All over America I find young people and adults with the same story. They know God's rules. They know they will eventually pay a big price for what they're doing. They promise themselves a thousand times that they will not go all the way the next time, but then they get into the situation and it happens again. It seems like victory over the temptation of sex constantly eludes them. It seems like an unsolvable problem. But it's not. There is a solution to this problem. It's simple, and yet so many people miss it by ten thousand miles. I am constantly amazed at how many people try to "live" the Christian life and "experience victory" over sin, but they have never really turned their lives over to Jesus and received him as Lord and Savior of their lives.

One night I was in Louisville, Kentucky. As I went back in the counseling area, a young lady about twenty-one came over and asked if we could talk for a moment. She looked at me and said, "Preacher, can a homosexual be filled with the Holy Spirit?"

I said, "What do you mean by being filled with the Holy Spirit?"

"I mean," she then said, "can a homosexual speak in tongues?"

"Are you a homosexual?" I asked.

"Yes."

"Do you speak in tongues?"

"Yes."

I asked her point blank, "Have you ever really turned your life over to Jesus Christ and received him as your

Let Him Put It All Together

personal Lord and Savior?"

"Oh, no," she said. "I have never done that."

As she went on, she kept telling me how much she wanted to be free from homosexuality. But she just wasn't strong and she would constantly fall back into that sin.

Now watch this closely. Here was a girl who had had some sort of freaky spiritual experience. She had psyched herself out and had spoken in some mumbo jumbo (*that is not speaking in tongues*), and because of that was convinced she was a Christian. And yet there had *never* been a time when she had honestly and completely turned her life over to Jesus. Then she was wondering why she never saw any victory and was becoming frustrated that God could not give her power over homosexuality.

This same thing happens in the lives of so many, many people who have had some kind of "spiritual experience," but have never genuinely been saved. Satan has succeeded in this generation to convince us of a thousand lies about salvation. Satan is so clever. If he cannot get you to do something wrong, he will get you to do something right in the wrong way and then kill you with that wrong; and you'll never know what hit you. And he continually does this with salvation. Satan wants us to believe if we will just join the right church; if we'll just get baptized; if we'll just get through confirmation, catechism, instruction, or new membership class; or he tries to tell us that if we'll just clean up our lives, then surely that will make us a Christian. But none of these things are true. Satan has lied again.

Dr. James Mahoney and I were driving away from a crusade one night when a young man ran up and knocked on the window of the car. "Preacher, I've got to talk to you. My girl is over in the counseling area, and she's really messed up about some things."

I said, "Look, meet me down at the church in just a few minutes, and bring your girl." He was about eighteen; she was sixteen. For the past eight months they had been leaving school, going over to her parents' home, going all the way, then getting back in the car and going back to school. The boy had made a commitment to Christ earlier in his life but was deeply out of fellowship with God. She, though she was a member of a church, never had really accepted Jesus as her Lord and Savior. I asked her if she was willing to give her life to Jesus. She said, "I don't believe enough."

I asked her, "Do you believe there is a God?"
"Yes."
"Do you believe Jesus is the Son of God?"
"Yes."
"Do you believe he died on the cross?"
"Yes."
"Do you believe God raised him from the dead?"
"Yes."
"You believe everything you need to believe. What is really bugging you?"

She said, "I just don't want to be a hypocrite."

Watch out, here's Satan again. See how clever he is? He had gotten this young lady so deeply trapped into sin that she felt like she could never really have victory. And even though she believed in Jesus, even though she accepted the fact that he is the Son of God, she was afraid that she couldn't change her life. She was afraid she couldn't quit doing the sex. Satan had convinced her that she was too weak to really have victory, and if she couldn't quit these things herself that God would never accept her. Let me say this as plainly and as explicitly and as dogmatically as I can. *You do not have to have victory over sin in your own power to be saved.* You do not have to quit anything to be saved! God doesn't expect you to clean up your life to be saved. God doesn't expect you to stop having illicit sex to be saved. In fact, God doesn't expect you to stop doing one single thing to be saved. God knows you can't quit doing these sins.

God knows that if it is left up to you that you will give in to every temptation that comes along. That is why Jesus said that a person's life is like a house. Before you give your life to Jesus, the devil lives inside that house. He is boss. You can decide that you are ready to get him out of there and clean up your life, so you do. You make a new resolution. You turn away from sin for a few minutes. You get inside this house that represents your life, and you really clean things up. You wash the walls and windows and sweep the floors, removing all but the severest stains, and it looks pretty good for a while.

But in a few days or a few weeks the devil comes back. He knocks on the door, peeks in the window, and aha! Nobody home. So he goes and gets a couple of his demons, kicks down the door, knocks out the windows, comes into your nice, clean house, and has a gay ole time, and you're worse off than before.

Isn't that the way it works? You decide you're really going to live it this time! You're going to quit doing this and quit doing that and start doing this and start doing that, but before you know it you're right back where you started, and really worse off than before because you think you've tried Jesus—and you really haven't tried him at all. You've tried to do it without him.

What Jesus wants is for you to bring him your house, dirt and all, and let him clean it up. He'll remove even the deepest stains with his blood, but then he'll live in that house. Then when the devil comes knocking on that door, Jesus will be there to answer, and he'll say, "Get lost, Satan! This one's mine!"

You say, how is that possible? All right, here's what happened. Two thousand years ago God became a human being. He became God in the flesh, a man filled with God, the Christ-man, 100 percent man, 100 percent God. The Bible says he was tempted in every way just as you and I are tempted. But because he was totally committed to the Father and let the power of God live in his life, he never sinned! Never! He was tempted, but he never broke the rules. Never! Now that's fantastic!

But you say, "That's okay, but after all, he was God! If I were God, I could overcome temptations, too."

You're right. You could! And that's exactly why God wants you to be "born again"—to have God-in-you—to start spiritually as his son so that you can have the same power available in your life that Jesus had in his. Now I know this is hard to believe. It is stranger than any science fiction book you will ever read, but it's true. I know, *personally*, that it is true.

Let's look at it this way. We call all the colors we can see "the spectrum." Red, orange, yellow, green, blue, indigo, and violet—that's the spectrum. Nothing unusual

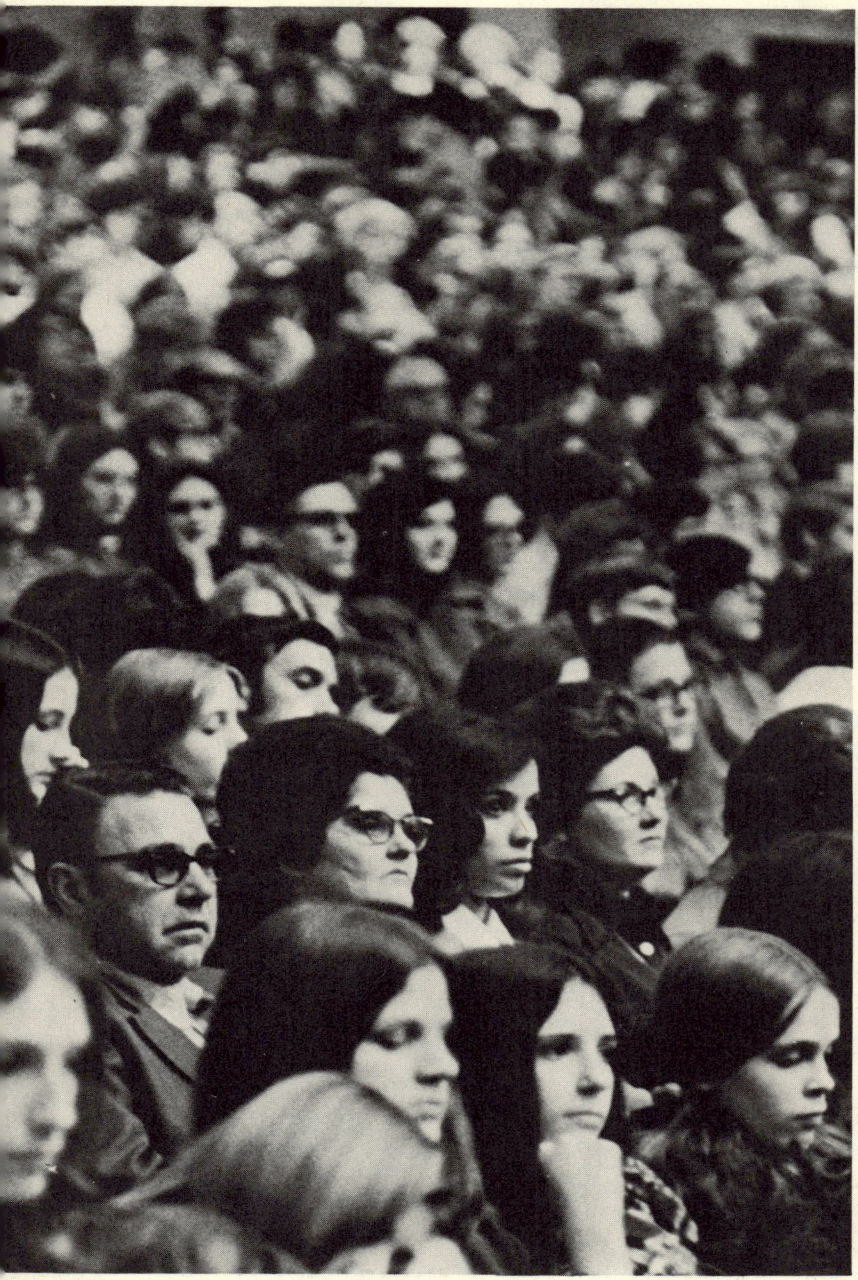

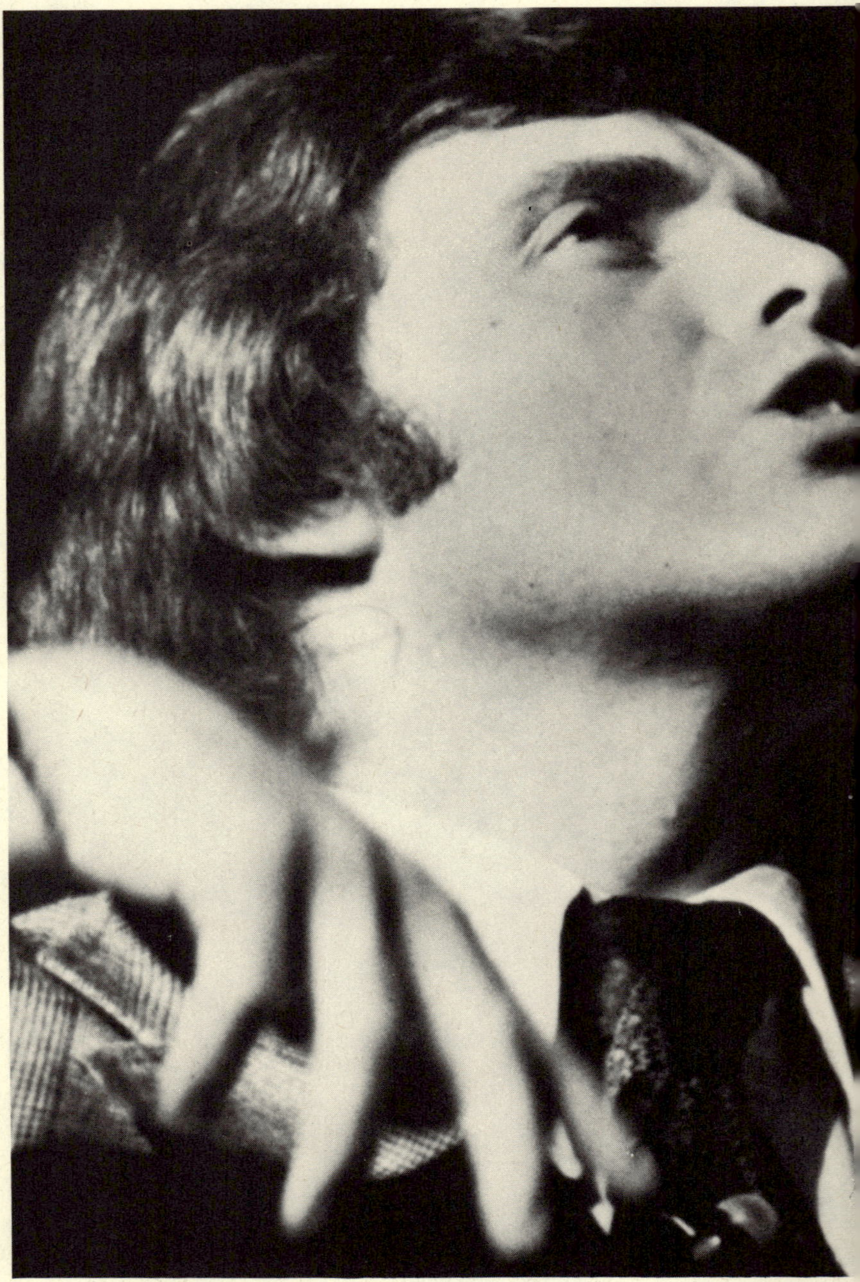

RICHARD HOGUE

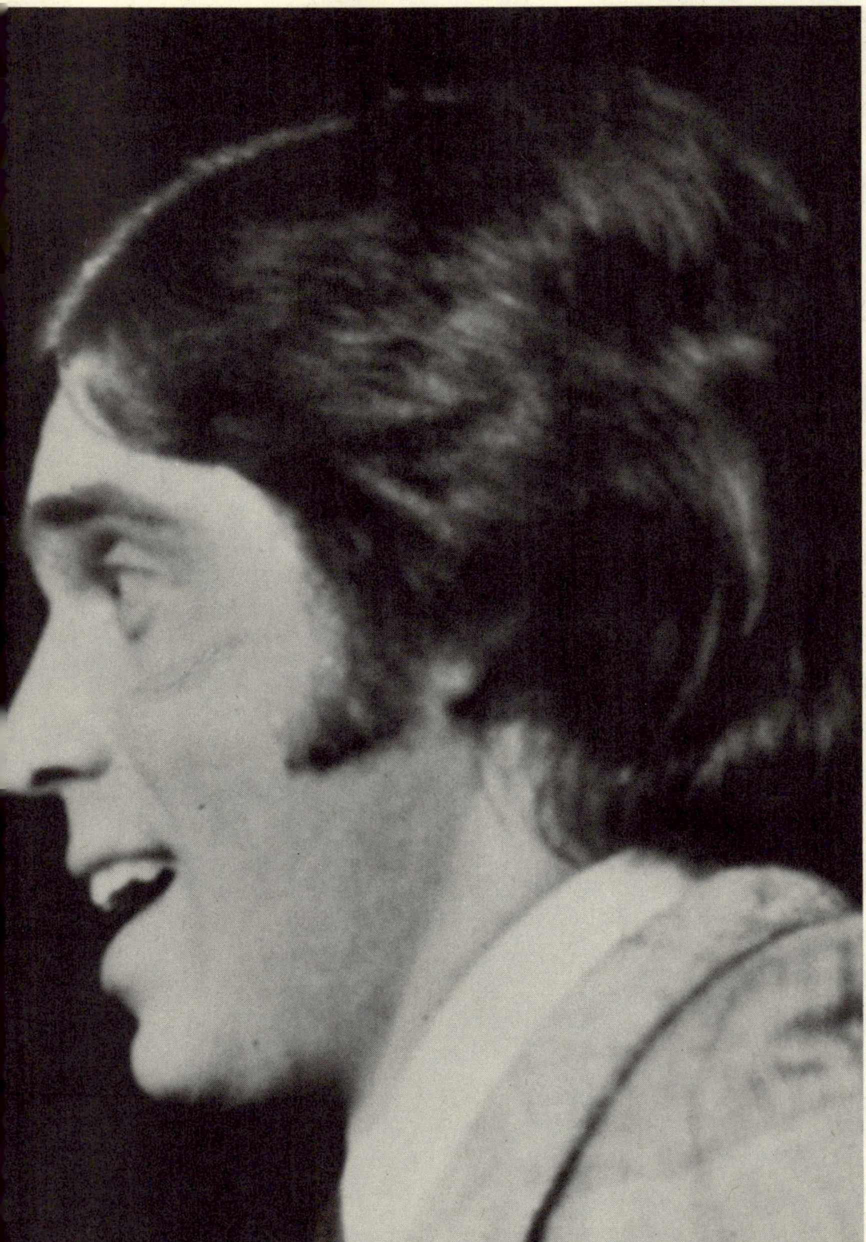

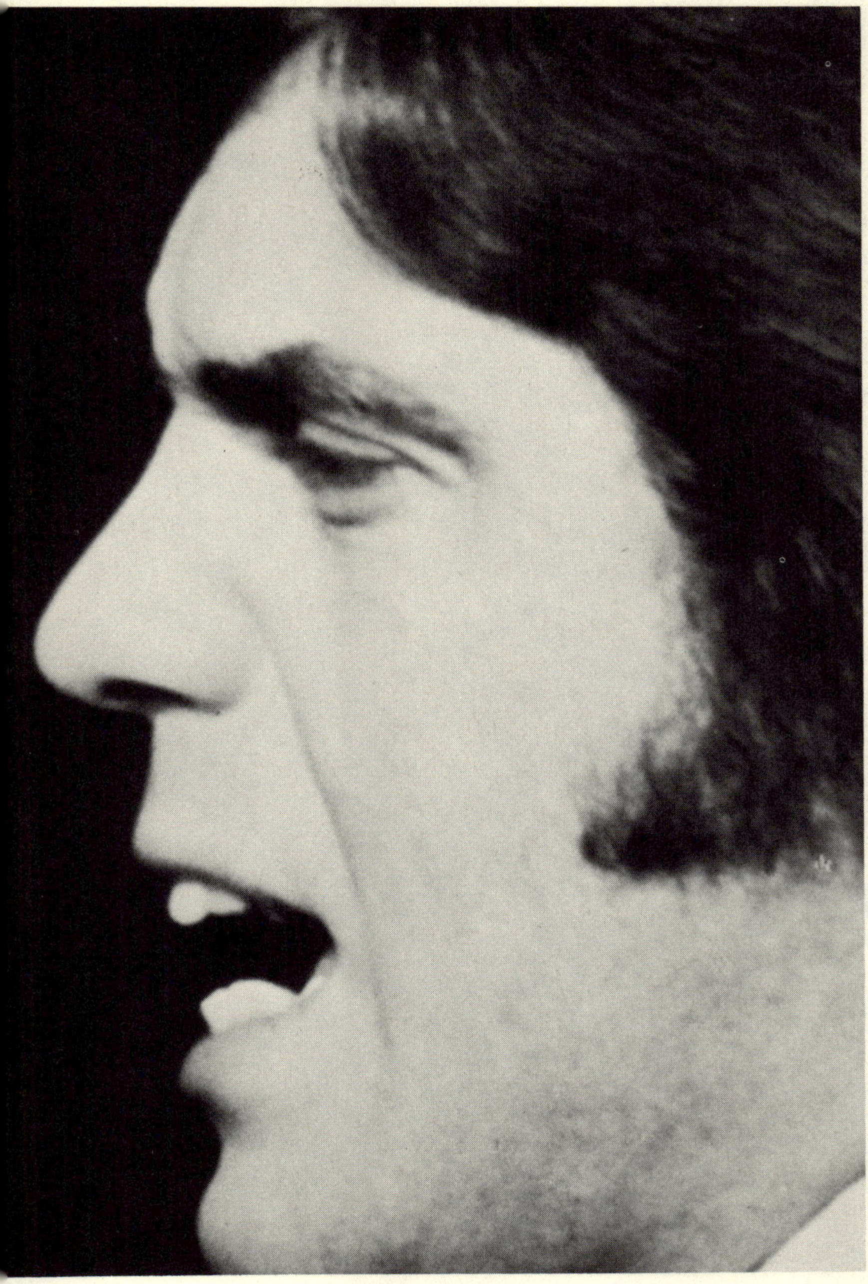

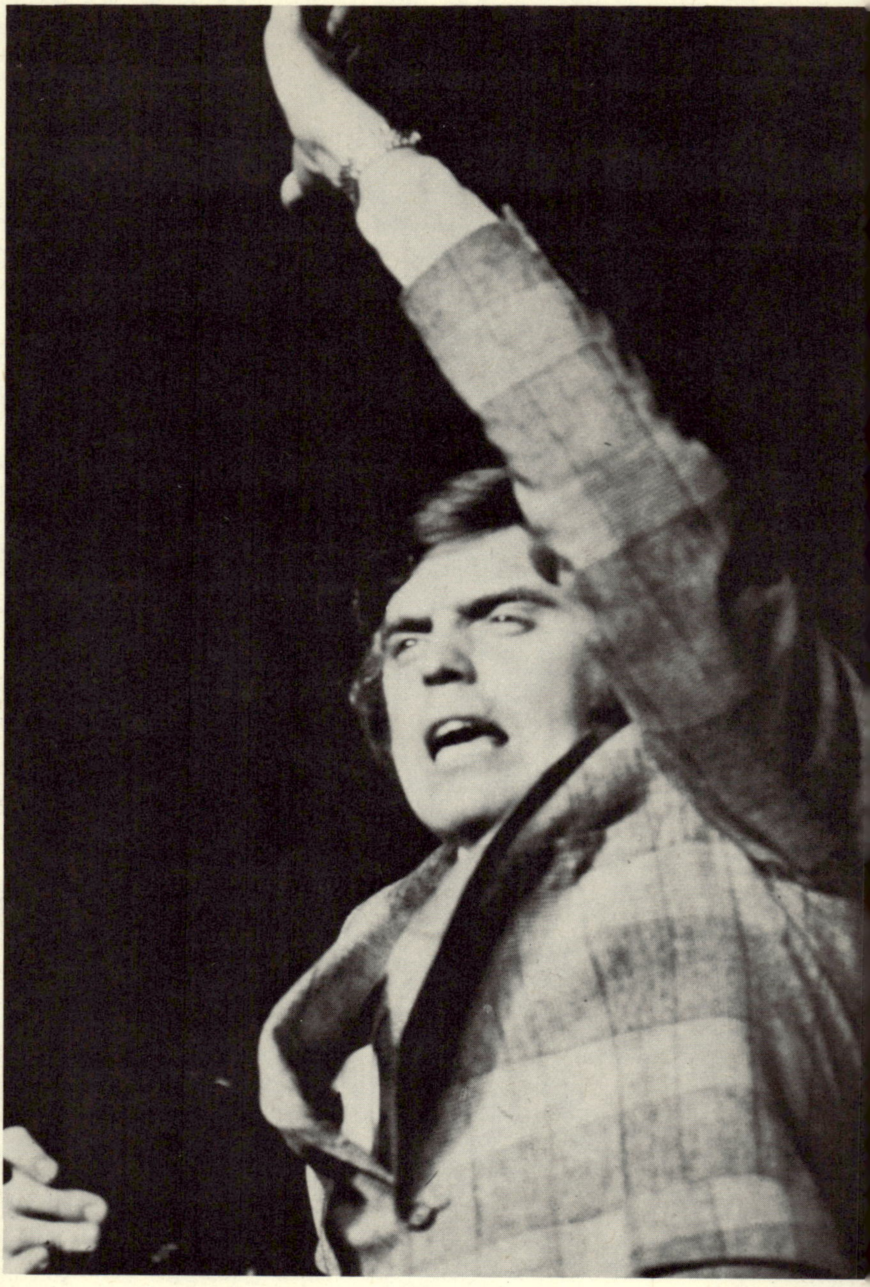

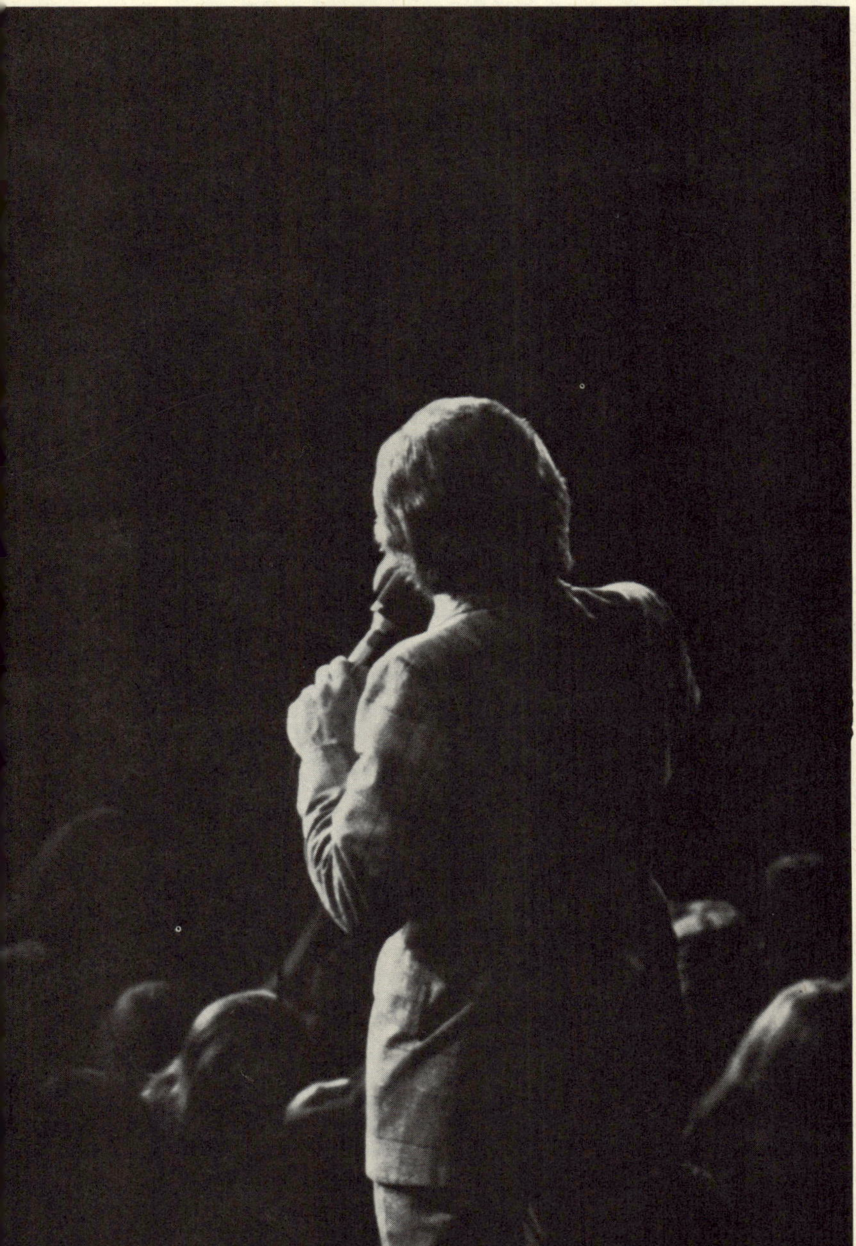

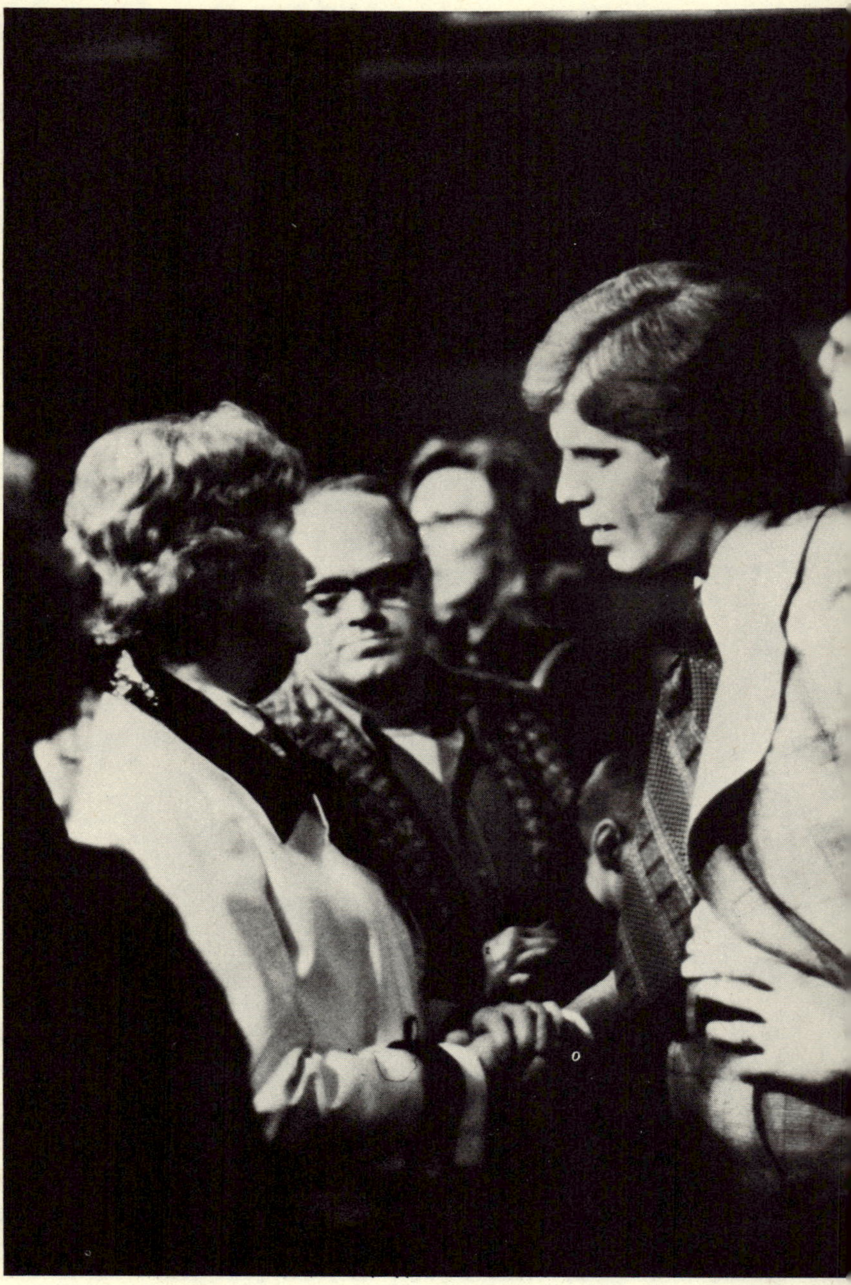

Let Him Put It all Together

about that. You can see them. But we also know that there are other waves of color that are *here* but are outside the *visible spectrum.* We can't see them. There is ultraviolet—beyond the violet. There is infrared—below the red. We can't see them because our eyes are not equipped for it. Now, get this. Jesus is the spectrum of God. When we talk about the spiritual, we are talking about something that is just as real as infrared, but it something you can't see with your eyes.

Or, you could take sound. The birds can hear sounds that humans can't hear. Dogs can hear sounds that we can't hear. Those waves are so frequent that they are beyond the top note the human ear can pick up. Actually, the sounds that we can hear cover only a few octaves. The other sounds we don't hear at all. We are not equipped for them.

Jesus is the octave of God. Most people never hear that note. But the good news is that Jesus can come into your range of hearing and feeling. It can happen. It is happening to people all over America and across the world, and it can happen to you. When it does, you will find the old temptations can be overcome!

Here's how it works. When you open up, God says to you, "Let's swap! You let me be the Lord (boss) of your life. You give me your mistakes. Shed them. Turn them all over to me. I'll put them all on my sin blackboard and take a big wet rag and wipe them off so you can forget them. Then I'll give you a Jesus life, a life filled with the Holy Spirit. I'll take your old life away and hand you a new life which will give you victory over every tough temptation you are going to face from now on. You die to your old self and start over full of me."

That is God's plan for us.

You say, "That's too super to be true. How does it work?"

When I went to college, I used to love to play tennis, but I was probably the worst tennis player in the whole school. The guy who lived across the hall from me, Ernie Botkin, was one of the best tennis players around. Well, every time we played, he would just beat the socks off me. Now just suppose that one day when we went out to play I could take Poncho Gonzales along with me—one of the world's greatest tennis players ever. Let's say I could cram ole Poncho down inside of me so that on the outside I still look like me but on the inside I'm really Poncho Gonzales. Pretty neat trick, *si?* At first I'd be playing by myself. I'd hit the ball, and heaven only knows where it would go, probably over the backstop or into the net. But then I'd finally turn ole Poncho loose, and I'd just beat the socks off Ernie! Ernie would rub his eyes and stare at me, drop his racket, and say, "Man, that sure looks like ole Hogue, but he sure doesn't play tennis like Hogue!"

Now that's silly, because we know that one man cannot live inside another man. But God can live in every man! And that's exactly what he wants to do! You may think God can't do that for you. You may think that you are already too hooked on sex, or dope, or success, or popularity, to get anything else into your mind. You are wrong. Jesus can crowd anything out. He has never been beaten yet.

Have you ever taken a magnifying glass and focused the sun's rays on a piece of wood? What happened? It burned a hole in the wood, didn't it? It gathered the heat of the sun, focused it in one tiny spot, and created a power that seemed impossible. It was like creating fire out of thin air. The same thing can happen in your life. The Holy Spirit is the power of Jesus focused into your life. He is so strong that he can burn a hole in the biggest temptation around.

Now, you may say, "I've already tried your prescription. I joined the church when I was ten years old."

But have you *really* tried it? Yes, you've joined the church—you got baptized—you tried to be a Christian—but have you ever really accepted Jesus as the Lord (boss) and Savior of your life? Has there ever been a moment when you genuinely committed your life unto Jesus—surrendered your will to his will? If there hasn't been, you are *not* a Christian. You may have joined every church in town—you may have been baptized 180 times—you may have gone through catechism, instruction, church membership, or confirmation classes—the whole bit—but if you've never turned your life over to Jesus, you're not a Christian. You've never really been saved.

That's what God is talking about in Romans 10:9-10 when he says you must believe not with the head, but with the heart—your belief must be more than mere mental assent; it must be a commitment of your life. It must be a commitment which says, "Jesus, I just can't do it—I just can't be my boss. You take control of my life. Fill me with your self and you *be* my victory. I give up and ask you to take charge!" Only when you do that have you really tried Jesus!

When you do that, he will enter your life by the person of the Holy Spirit, forgive you of your sin, and start being your personal victory over the temptations which Satan throws at you.

But one word of caution: Even with God in your life now, the devil will still frequently try to get back in, so be on the lookout for him. C. S. Lovett, in his excellent book *Dealing with the Devil,* has given a prescription for a satanic intruder control system which goes something like this; I recommend it:

1) *Keep the lights on.* Knowledge and insight about how and where Satan is likely to strike is the best protection from him.

2) *Watch for him.* Satan usually comes disguised as SELF, so you need to ask the Holy Spirit to nudge you so that you'll think of the devil, instead of thinking that this is what *you* really want to do and "it won't really matter." Try to catch him early before he can do his damage.

3) *Install an alarm system.* You do this by admitting that you yourself can do nothing, then speaking to Satan in Jesus' name, demanding that he leave your mind. (He's not afraid of us puny human beings—and we can't whip him—but he is afraid of Jesus. He knows that Jesus can overthrow his strangle-hold on our minds and send him hopping.)

4) *Use your weapon.* Our weapon is the Bible—God's Word is our sword. Even Jesus used a verbal statement to drive Satan away. He said, "Satan be gone!" And notice that Jesus always followed that with, "For it is written . . ." He would quote God's Word for that particular situation.

We must do the same thing. We must say, "Satan! In

Let Him Put It All Together

the name of the Lord Jesus, go away! Be gone!" Then quote what you know to be God's Word for that particular situation. (It doesn't have to be an *exact quotation*—just the truth of what you know God says in his Word.) If you don't replace the devil's suggestions with God's suggestions, you leave yourself open and empty like that house.

There is no magic in this formula. The magic is in the Holy Spirit—in his power. The formula works like a light switch. One touch on your part and a whole power station is at your disposal. One bit of resistance by you, and God does the rest. Yes, it's true that the Bible says, "Greater is he that is in you than he that is in the world" (1 John 4:4). But so many forget that it also says, "Resist the devil and he will flee from you" (James 4:7). That means that *we* have to do *something*. We have to make some move to *resist* before God can move in to help us. God never forces us to do anything, even after we have claimed his Holy Spirit. We must go first. We must push the button. But lift that switch—say the word—and WHAM. All God's machinery goes to work for you.

Wallace Hamilton, in his book *Where Now Is Thy God?*, tells about a man who stood up in an Alcoholics Anonymous meeting and described his conversion. He said that he had a very intricate watch, and when something went wrong with it, he tried to fix it himself. But that didn't work out too well. So after that he decided to take it to a watchmaker who knew all about the inner workings of watches. Then one day it dawned on him that he had treated his own life like that watch. He had tried to fix it himself, and he couldn't. "And there came a day," he said, "when I realized my only hope was to go humbly to my Maker and ask him to fix me. And I did. And he did."

That's what God can do in your life when you are willing by faith to turn it all over to him—*your Maker*— the one who knows everything that makes you tick.

Jesus knows the solution to the puzzle you are facing in your life—and he's ready to put the pieces together for you—if you'll turn them all over to him!

8

"The Morning After Blues"

We were in a New Mexico military town. After the service David Smith, our counseling director, came to me and said, "Richard, you have to talk to this guy. He won't open up to anyone else."

When I got to the counseling area, this young airman about twenty-seven was leaning over his chair, his head in his hands, weeping. He looked up at me and then immediately back down. "I really love her; I don't know why I did it," he said. "Did what?" Slowly he started to tell the story—almost a phrase at a time. "When I first came out here, my wife didn't come with me. She was teaching school where we were and couldn't leave. One night I was out and I met this chick. She just really seemed to understand my loneliness. I told her I was married. She said that was okay.

"Well then, preacher, for about the next month until my wife got here, I had sex with this girl about every night. And man, I really love my wife. I just kinda fell into this thing, and there seemed to be no way out, and man I really love my wife. I just can't tell you how bad I feel. I have asked God to forgive me and really *think* he did, but man the guilt is about to drive me up the wall. I know my wife would kill me if she knew. It would really tear her up. There is no way she would forgive me. There is just no way. I feel guilty and dirty. What am I going to do?"

It never seems to fail. Of all the problems we deal with, none brings with it more guilt than the misuse of sex. Even when people have been heavy into alcohol—or stealing, cheating, jealously—you name it, even those who have been experimenting with drugs can somehow get out of that particular area of sin without knowing deep feelings of guilt. But sex involves every area of a person's life— physical, mental, and spiritual. It is amazing the deep scars and feelings of guilt that a person retains for years and years throughout his life because of the misuse of sex.

Now some guilt of course is good, because we are all indeed guilty of rebellion against God, doing our thing instead of his. We are all born into sin since the fall of Adam. Adam was created perfect, but the rest of us were born of Adam after he had sinned—with a fallen, selfish nature. As Romans 3:23 says, "We have all sinned and come short of the glory of God." And when you break one of God's laws (unless you harden your heart through continued disobedience and refusal of repentance), there is going to be a point of sorrow and conviction and guilt because you are guilty of that sin.

In fact, one of the ministries of the Holy Spirit, the Scriptures say, is conviction. He brings about sorrow of sin and leads us to repent and turn back to God. Without realization of sin and accompanying guilt, one would never realize his need of a Savior and would never be saved. Now I am really not afraid or concerned that you will overemphasize the conviction you feel when God deals with your sin through guilt. What concerns me is that Satan is going to use the area of guilt to destroy you with something for which God has already forgiven you. Satan uses the emotion of guilt as a powerful tool to do two things—to defeat and neutralize the Christian, his enemy, and to keep the person who has never given his life to Christ from making that original commitment.

One night on a plane coming back from Los Angeles, my associate Steve Brittain, was talking to one of the stewardesses. He sensed a deep feeling of guilt about some of the things that had happened in her life. As she started letting the story out, all the details became very evident. Her guilt had driven her to mental and spiritual masochism. About four years ago, she had become pregnant. Because she was not married, that pregnancy had been aborted. This had haunted her for the past four years of her life. She felt so bad about the abortion—the killing of the child—as she called it. It had driven her to dope, heavy alcohol, and from one illicit affair to another as a way to degrade herself—to get even with herself—for the abortion. Every day she would beg and plead with God to forgive her for that abortion. The guilt was literally driving her to a mental breakdown.

This guilt was nothing less than the working of Satan in her life. It was not God trying to convict her of her sin. This was Satan abusing and accusing her and trying to destroy her life. Satan had convinced her that God did not love her. He had told her that her sin was too bad. God could not forgive her. Satan did not force her to believe these lies, but the entire philosophy of guilt came directly from his mind to her mind in the form of suggestion, though she never recognized it as Satan. Thus her guilt had given Satan a handle through her emotions which he was now almost able to control at will, driving her from one sin to another.

How many hundreds of people are just this way? Satan has their personalities so controlled that they cannot respond to love or even return real love. Oh, they put up a fair front, a facade, but it is only a covering for the deep pangs of guilt. And this is exactly how Satan works. Once a person knowingly sins, the Holy Spirit convicts him of that sin quickly to bring repentance. Satan immediately moves in to block him from relating the sin to the cross and accepting available forgiveness. He has two methods. Man cannot live with guilt, so Satan suggests to man two ways of dealing with it—self-justification and self-condemnation. Either way there is a loss of fellowship with God—alienation, estrangement. Self-justification results in estrangement because deep down the person knows the truth, he knows those sins are not justifiable, and he knows God knows. He heaps sin on top of sin so he feels farther from God than ever. Self-condemnation brings about estrangement because the individual gets to believing he has gone too far to be forgiven. He thinks either God can't forgive him or he won't forgive him.

I remember even back in high school when witnessing to a girl, a friend of mine, this comment: "Well frankly, I just don't believe in God any more." "I've tried to pray, but my prayers don't get above the ceiling." Now here was the example of a young girl whose guilt had made her feel so far apart from God that she had finally decided he just wasn't even there.

Another young woman, married for eight years now, told her pastor a story that had been making her feel guilty for years. She was afraid it was ruining her marriage. When she was a teenager, she ran around with the wrong crowd. She got into a car with four boys one evening. She knew them, and didn't think it would hurt. But they drove around just having fun and started drinking. They all began to be a little drunk, including herself. She said they began to joke about having sex with her. She resisted their advances. They said they would rape her if she didn't submit. She really didn't believe they would but she let them do it anyway. All of them. She had been living with this scar in her mind for all these years. She was afraid to tell her husband, and yet she wanted to be honest with him. She was miserable, and wondered if she would ever get over it. Now when she had sex with her husband she felt dirty and guilty.

Any guilt you have about sin—after you have repented and confessed that sin to Jesus and received his forgiveness through faith in his promises—is of Satan. And if you are going to have real victory over this haunting feeling of guilt, there are some things you must know about God and how he deals with sin. There are some sin concepts which need to be cleared up in your mind. Many people believe God is some sort of strange Spirit in the sky who carries around a big club. Every time you step out of line, he knocks your brains out. That is a lie of Satan. Some people have been waiting for years for God to let them have it and get even with them for their sin. Something bad happens to you, and Satan says "Uh huh. There's

God letting you have it for something you did five years ago. You never will live that down."

Whether you are a Christian or a lost person, the basic misconception which Satan has repeatedly implanted into your mind is that God is mad at you. And Satan uses all of your guilt and all of your fear to get you mad at God. Or maybe you don't get mad. You say, "I know I deserve it." But the realization of your unworthiness makes you feel like you are a million miles away from God. Satan convinces you that your sin has made God completely out of touch, and he wins another victory. He attacks bigger and bolder than ever while you are not communicating with the only one who can protect you.

Satan has a vicious trap he delights in using on Christians. It works like this. You have special areas of weakness in your old sin nature at which Satan loves to keep pounding away until he can catch you not depending on the Holy Spirit, and thus you sin. You ask God for forgiveness and feel better, but then it happens again. You ask God for forgiveness again, but you feel a little guilty for having so little will power. After Satan gets you to sin in this area *again,* you feel so unworthy you hate even to ask God to forgive you. But you vow one final time never again! If he'll just forgive you one more time. Whamo! Satan has you right where he wants you—trying to please God in the power of the flesh. The harder you try, the more you fail.

Finally, after continual defeat in this spiritual battle, you are too ashamed to even come to God's threshold of mercy and ask for forgiveness. And here comes old Satan the accuser in his favorite role. "You have vowed again and again you will quit. You haven't. So God's not going to listen to you anymore. He's not going to believe you again! You've sinned too much, you've come too far. God won't forgive you this time." Or, for smarter individuals, he has another line. "He may forgive you, but you will sure miss out on what he had in store for you." And then, all of a sudden, in your mind you become from then on a second-rate Christian.

The real issue is not whether God will believe you or your promises to him, but whether you believe in God's promises of forgiveness and power. All Satan has to do is get your eyes off the issue. Are you continually going to dwell on self (even though it is the putting down of self), or are you going to look to Jesus? Are you going to trust him for inner strength—his strength—to overcome temptation?

One of the main reasons I think we do not believe in God's promise of forgiveness is because we do not understand his provision for forgiveness. If there is one clear point I would like to get across to you in this chapter, it is that God is not hacked off at you because of your sin. In fact, the exact opposite is true. The Bible says that God so loved you that he gave his only begotten Son (John 3:16). The Scripture says "Behold what manner of love the Father hath bestowed upon us, that we should be called the sons of God" (1 John 3:1). God loves us so much that he turns the curse into a blessing (Deut. 23:5). God loves you so much that even in the middle of your sin, God still loves you and he wants to forgive you.

The Bible shows us that God hates sin. He detests sin but loves the sinner. "While we were yet sinners Christ died for us" (Rom. 5:8). That is why Jesus came to die, to provide a way for God to kill, to destroy sin, but to give us life. Jesus came to reconcile us to God. In the original Greek New Testament that word for reconcile is *apokatallasso*. Now it is completely different from what we usually think of as the word reconciliation; that two people or groups get together and get their differences ironed out. This Greek word means that only one party is at odds with the other. The other is not mad at all. God was in Christ and reconciled the world unto himself (2 Cor. 5:19). He did not need to reconcile himself with the world, because he had nothing to clear up. So when Jesus died, he made it possible for man to be totally clean and pure before God. "That we might become the righteousness of God" (2 Cor. 5:21). And you can't get any cleaner, purer, holier, or more righteous than that!

Now Satan knows far better than you what Jesus has done, and he knows the fantastic love God has for the world. But this is one thing Satan does not want the world to know about. In fact he is going to do all he can to keep you from really living in this victory. That is why he wants you to keep your eyes on your sin instead of on the cross. Because the cross is what really wipes out your sins and guilt.

When Jesus died, he took all our sins to the cross with him. Every sin that everyone has ever lived or committed, he took to the cross. The Scriptures say that "He who knew no sin *became* sin" (2 Cor. 5:21). In other words, he became the very thing that God hates and wants to destroy. He willingly accepted what is detestable to the Father. Think of it. And the Bible says God spared him not.

Jesus was God's sacrifice prepared before the foundation of the world. You see, at the cross things did not go wrong for God, they went right. God sent his Son and gave him to the world to die for our sins on the cross. The cross was God's way of taking away your guilt, your shame, your sins, so that you do not have to live with guilt if you will accept the fact that God has forgiven you. God showed the world how much he hated sin on the cross. But he showed how much he loves the sinner by allowing his only Son to be the brunt of sin. That is what 1 John 2:1-2 is talking about when it says, "If anyone sins we have an advocate with the Father, Jesus Christ the righteous and he himself is the propitiation for our sins and not for ours only, but for the whole world."

Propitiation means to turn away deserved wrath. The Bible says, "God took all his hostilities against us and our sin and nailed them to the cross" (Col. 2:14). Jesus, in his death, defeated sin and Satan (Col. 2:15).

And think of the audacity of Satan, who wants to try to get you to think that your sin is more unjust than Jesus' death. That is why you feel guilty. Now I don't care how immoral and decadent you have been. Nothing you could ever do could be as unjust as the death of Jesus on the cross. Remember, "He who knew no sin became sin." You may be assured that God would never have allowed Christ to make the sacrifice if it were not greater than all your sins. But Satan never wants you to experience that love and sacrifice that Jesus made, and if he can, he will keep you constantly in that merry-go-round of sin. You will sin, you will feel guilty, your guilt leads you to get mad at God for holding the sin against you, and then you sin more because you say, "He won't forgive me anyway. What does it matter, God doesn't love me."

Listen, that doesn't make sense!

God wants to forgive you more than you want to be forgiven. You didn't ask Jesus to die. It was God's plan in the first place. I purposely repeat: Satan's biggest endeavor is to keep your eyes off the cross, to make you discount or minimize the terrific price paid for your sin. The cross is the continuing basis for God's acceptance and forgiveness of you. Learning what Jesus accomplished through the cross is the most important truth your mind can ever absorb because that is what the Bible is talking about when it says, "You shall know the truth, and the truth shall set you free" (John 8:32). Freedom—freedom from all sin and its bondage. Freedom—from guilt. Freedom—that brings about peace. Freedom—that brings about joy. Freedom—that brings about happiness, true life itself. So look at the cross one more time and try to grasp all that it holds for you.

Don't ever minimize the price Jesus paid for your sin to set you free. The "Treehouse Club," a new religious TV program of the Sesame Street variety, reports that the average child that watches TV regularly sees approximately seventy people murdered on TV per week. This tends to make us quite indifferent to death and consequently to just kind of pass over the death of Jesus on the cross. I hear a lot of "so what, lots of good guys get killed and some do it trying to save other people." But *wait a minute!* This is *not* another man—this is God.

Now I don't know about you—yes, I do, too. If it were you or I, either one, just suppose we created something and had the power to bring it to life and that thing spat in our face, turned on us, and said, "I'm going to do *my* thing." Then it went over to our enemies' camp to join forces and add support to them. You or I would say, "You think so, huh? Well I've got news for you, *smash!*" And that would be the end of that. Now grasp this. Jesus, the Bible says, did the creating. He flung the stars and the planets into space, but more importantly *created you.* The same creator God—who knows and enjoys the heaven of this universe—left that glory and splendor and came to this cursed, fallen planet. He became one of us and experienced its physical and mental turmoil. He allowed the people he had made to kill him.

Now let's look more closely at what Christ went through. The Vatican, a few years ago, prepared an article for all the major newspapers, reporting the most up-to-date findings by combined Bible scholars and archaeologists on the facts surrounding Jesus' death. It said there are seven types of pain in the world and Jesus experienced all of them.

The first thing—long before he ever got to the cross—was the brutal scourging. This was by a long leather whip with separate strands in which were tied pieces of rock, bone, and metal. The Vatican report stated that the usual beating given with this weapon consisted of thirty stipes, but that Jesus was beaten close to 119 times. No wonder the Bible says that his back was laid bare. He was beaten to the bone. Then, of course, there was the crown of thorns pressed upon his brow. A wooden cane was mockingly given to him as a scepter and then taken away to beat his head with and drive the thorns in further.

The splintery cross, laid upon Jesus' back for him to carry, weighed hundreds of pounds. It had to be tied to his arms and his back. His repeated falls while walking those tortuous steps to Calvary had to be stopped only with his knees and face. There was nothing else to stop his fall. When they reached the hill, of course, there was the well known nailing of the hands and feet to the cross with six- to nine-inch spikes lodged between the bones so that they would not rip right through the flesh. And then the cross was slung into the socket, leaving the Son of God hanging in a slow process of suffocation.

You see, that is the real death method of the crucifixion—the collapsed lungs of the hung position resulting in slow, gradual suffocation. The crucified would always push up against the nails in his feet to get some air into his lungs; and then as he collapsed again, the air of course would be forced out with pressure. That's why after so long, the soldiers would finally come around and break a person's knees so that death could come more quickly. But as was prophesied thousands of years before the coming of the Messiah, none of Jesus' bones were broken. Jesus was allowed to suffer a lengthy nine hours on the cross.

Of course, there is no way to comprehend how hideous the filthy spitting and mocking must have been. Can you imagine what it must have been like to have the very little people—the puny little people—you created and love so much taunting you with, "If you're the Son of God, come down off the cross." And knowing you *could* come down at any moment! (Boy, would that have freaked them out! It would have scared them to death.)

In fact, the Bible says ten thousand angels were ready in heaven with swords drawn, begging and pleading to come wipe this planet into oblivion. But Jesus said, "No,

I must face this alone." He knew there was no other way for man to be saved. He knew you and I would spend eternity in hell unless he experienced it for us. God dying for the ones he made and the very sins we committed against him. It doesn't make sense. There is no way our finite minds can comprehend the infinite love of the infinite God.

Jesus went to hell for us. Whatever else hell is and whatever else Jesus experienced, he had to experience complete separation from God and isolation from everyone else. On the cross he cried out, "My God, my God, why hast thou forsaken me?"

It's funny what will sometimes bring an incident into our grasp to help us begin to understand what Jesus went through. Something has to bring it within our realm of experience, which is usually so shallow.

Last year when my wife was pregnant with our second child, Jeremy, we lost our little eight-inch, four-pound, chocolate poodle, Jacob. He was in California with us for a crusade, and a vet overdosed him with a rabies vaccine. Marilyn had to fly to Houston for a doctor's appointment and couldn't get him to come out from under the bed because he was so sick. She had to make a plane and I had to make one for another part of the country, so our pastor friend said that he would get Jacob, take him to the vet, get him well, and then send him on to Houston for us.

Reluctantly, but having no choice, Marilyn caught her flight and made her appointment. The next evening I had to call her and tell her that Jacob had died at the veterinarian's office. They had thought he was fine but found him dead in a cell the next morning. Well, as our minds will allow, Marilyn coped with it pretty well at first, busy with other things and not allowing herself to dwell on it. But at about 2:00 A.M. that night, trying to go to sleep in a bed that usually included a little brown dog curled up inside her knees, was just too much. And she began to sob.

Marilyn said she wasn't crying so much for the fact that Jacob was gone and she missed him as for the thought of how lonely and frightened he must have been. He had to be pulled out from under the bed in a strange place by strangers and taken to a strange vet and treated in a strange cell, wondering where we were—and dying all alone. Oddly enough, it was at that moment that it hit her full force what God must have felt at the crucifixion. She thought to herself, "Marilyn, here you are crying over a little dog." "Think what almighty God must have gone through when he had to turn his back on his only Son and allowed him not just to die, but to be horribly tortured and sacrificed." "And not just amidst strangers, but enemies—terribly, terribly alone." For the first time, she not only began to fathom the hideous loneliness Christ had to feel, but the unbearable grief and sorrow God the Father must have felt to allow it.

Then, as if all this were not enough, there is the guilt. You think *you* live with guilt! Christ, in dying for our sins, experienced the weight of guilt your sins produce plus that of all the world. Now get serious and think on this. That sin that has been haunting and gnawing at you, put Jesus through the same mental torture. And not only your sin, but those of the worst criminals, the biggest rebels, every sin ever committed. Can you imagine the weight? Unbearable! But think even further. Here is one who never has *known* sin— *never* known sin—all of a sudden bearing all these hideous crimes. Guilt brings torture to anyone who indulges in some sin, but the terrible impact Christ must have experienced! And to actually be innocent—blameless in his own life.

How many times do children and adults alike delight in telling about spankings they didn't deserve or things they were falsely blamed for. All of us can usually think of several examples of times we were unjustly accused for something. And blame is always hard to take, let alone when we are innocent! Some times it stays with us like a scar no matter how many times we may have missed other punishment richly deserved. But Christ was not just falsely accused. "Christ also suffered. He died once for the sins of all of us guilty sinners, although he himself was innocent of any sin at any time, that he might bring us safely home to God" (1 Pet. 3:18). This is why Jesus could say right before bowing his head and committing his Spirit, "It is finished." The total price for your sin was paid in full. All the physical, all the mental, and all the spiritual debt. The sacrifice itself was complete. And the value of the life of the one sacrificed means another will never be necessary.

The only real issue is whether you accept or reject this provision for forgiveness. It doesn't seem fair, and it isn't. It's not an even exchange. That's why many do not believe God's offer even after they understand it. We expect God to treat us the way we treat him.

We have lied to God repeatedly. So Satan comes and says, "Why should God be true to you?"

In the end, everything goes back to the same old temptation—the very first, the original, popping up again—to *disbelieve* God. But it's up to you. Satan has no grounds to hassel and control your mind with guilt unless you give it to him. So start *today*—right now—taking God at his word. And realize and *claim* a forgiveness which is *already* a fact!

9

Admit It, Quit It, and Forget It

"Jesus, this woman was caught in the very act of adultery. Moses' law says to kill her. What about it?" They were trying to trap him into saying something they could use against him, but Jesus stooped down and wrote in the dust with his finger. They kept demanding an answer, so he stood up again and said, "All right, hurl the stones at her until she dies. But only he who never sinned may throw the first!" Then he stooped down again and wrote some more in the dust. And the Jewish leaders slipped away one by one, beginning with the eldest, until only Jesus was left in front of the crowd with the woman. Then Jesus stood up again and said to her, "Where are your accusers? Didn't even one of them condemn you?"

"No sir," she said.

And Jesus said, "Neither do I. Go and sin no more" (John 8:4-11, Living Bible).

What? What did Jesus say? "Neither do I condemn you"? A simple "Go and don't do it any more"? I mean, after all, this woman was a prostitute. I mean she was caught in the very act of adultery. I mean, I thought Jesus would really let this chick have it, but instead his actions are more to help her put the pieces back together instead of to destroy her. Now don't take this wrong. Jesus was in no way going "light" on this sin, but instead, "heavy" on forgiveness. In this incident, we see the most classic example of how God deals with sexual sin and how overwhelmingly willing he is to forgive.

But to talk about God's forgiveness you must first of all remember that in the life of a person who has never really committed himself to Christ, God is not really interested in forgiving the various *sins* of a person's life. He is extremely interested in forgiving the *sin*—that *sin* which makes a person separated from God and causes all the other *sins* a person commits. That sin is the same sin that we talked about earlier in the life of Satan, the sin of rebellion. It is the sin of rebellion that says, "I'll be my own God, and I'll call my own shots." You will never have your *sins* forgiven until you allow God to forgive you of this basic *sin* of rebellion and receive Christ as your Lord and Savior.

Once you've done that, once you've really committed your life to Christ and that old sin of rebellion has been forgiven, then you're in a totally new ball game. And the way God deals with your sin as a Christian is completely different. We find it in 1 John 1:9. God says, "If we confess our sins, he is faithful and just to forgive us our sins and to cleanse us from all unrighteousness." In *essence,* God says, Admit it, quit it, and forget it. But it is imperative that we realize exactly what God is saying. Notice that 1 John 1:9 does not say, "If we *confess,*" but it says, "If we *confess* our *sins.*" There is a big difference.

"Confession of sin" involves two things—two attitudes,

two spirits—a spirit of admission and a spirit of repentance. Simple confession means nothing. But to confess something as a sin means admitting it is wrong and admitting what is right. It is agreeing with God and agreeing with an attitude about your sin. Someone can confess something but not really feel it is wrong or experience any remorse for it. And a person can even confess something and admit it is wrong, but not be willing to quit. That is not genuine repentance which true confession of sin includes. True confession of sin is admitting you have sinned and agreeing with God you must turn from that sin.

Many Christians sin sexually, then get on their knees and confess having done it, but they never confess it as a sin. Some admit it is wrong but just list off their sins to God or a priest to get the slate clean—no repentance is involved. That is why many people never experience the joy that God has for them. They aren't really "confessing their sins." But when we agree with God about our sin, we put ourselves in position to call on God for his strength to turn from that sin, and beyond that, to trust him for the victory.

Now from the moment of salvation, when we are "born again," "born of the Spirit," our *relationship* as "sons of God" and "heirs with Christ" is established and nothing can change it.

"Ye have received the Spirit of adoption . . . the Spirit itself beareth witness with our spirit, that we are the children of God: And if children, then heirs; heirs of God, and joint-heirs with Christ" (Rom. 8:15-18). "And because of what Christ did, all you others, who heard the Good News about how to be saved, and trusted Christ, were marked as belonging to Christ by the Holy Spirit, who long ago had been promised to all of us Christians. His presence within us is God's guarantee that he really will give us all that he promised; and the Spirit's seal upon us means that God has already purchased us and that he guarantees to bring us to himself" (Eph. 1:13-14, Living Bible). So that "neither death, nor life, nor angels, nor principalities, nor powers, nor things present, nor things to come, nor height, nor death, nor any other creature, shall be able to separate us from the love of God, which is in Christ Jesus our Lord" (Rom. 8:38-39).

Christ himself says, "I give them eternal life and they shall never perish. No one shall snatch them away from me, for my Father has given them to me, and he is more powerful than anyone else, so no one can kidnap them from me" (John 10:28-29). "So there is now no condemnation awaiting those who belong to Christ Jesus" (Rom. 8:1). But in order to enjoy perfect *fellowship* with God, we must keep our sins confessed. Even though a Christian's sins were forgiven when Jesus died on the cross, unconfessed sins keep you from really *enjoying* your relationship with God and experiencing the power he offers to whip them. Why let sin which is already forgiven by what Jesus did on the cross defeat you when a simple "admit it and quit it" will give you the joy and power God so wants you to have?

At this point God says: Forget it, for the forgiveness itself is already a settled fact. If you confess it as a sin (admit to it and turn from it), you might as well forget it, for God does. In fact, the Bible says, "He removes our sins as far as the east is from the west and remembers them no more" (Ps. 10-3:12). And in Isaiah 43:25, God says, "I, yes, I alone am he who blots away your sins for my own sake and will never think of them again." The very literal translation of the Greek verb tenses in 1 John 1:9 further proves this. It says in actuality, "If we keep on confessing our sins, he is faithful and just to have forgiven us our sins and to have cleansed us from all unrighteousness." The forgiveness is already accomplished. It is finished. All we have to do is claim it.

It was finished on the cross. When Jesus was on the cross right before he died, the Bible says that he cried out with a loud voice saying, "It is finished." What was finished? The thing that had to be done so you could have all your sins forgiven was finished. Because of what Jesus did on the cross, no matter what you've done, no matter how perverse and sinful your life has been—you may have sacked out with every person that has come along, been heavy in sexual sin, prostituted your body—it doesn't matter. God will forgive all of that stuff if you will simply confess it as a sin.

You say, "But I just don't see how that can be? I just don't understand how the death of Jesus can wipe out my sin (or sins)?" Okay, let's look at the beauty of God's master plan with which he accomplished all this. First of all, the Bible says (1 Cor. 6:17), "If you give yourself to the Lord, you and Christ are joined together as one person" (Living Bible). Therefore, when God sees you, instead of seeing you, he sees Jesus. He no longer sees all your filthy sin; instead, he sees the righteousness of Jesus. And this is the continuing basis for your forgiveness. It doesn't depend on your *performance* but rather your *position,* your position in Christ, whom God accepts perfectly. You see, the Bible says that long before the world was made, God chose us to be his very own through what Jesus would do for us. He decided to make us holy in his eyes without a single fault so we could stand before him covered with his love. That's the key word—"covered." We are "holy and blameless" (Col. 1:22) because we are covered, covered by his blood.

A few months ago, I was listening to Billy Graham preach his sermon, "The Blood." I listened to the unbelievable detail of all the Old Testament sacrifices and how a blood sacrifice was specified for sin.

I must admit I left there with real questions in my mind. I kept saying to myself, "why blood"? Dr. Graham had said that because we are in the blood line of Adam, it is through this blood that we inherited our sin nature. A blood sacrifice is for payment of our sins. He further showed that the blood is that cleansing part of the human that cleans the body of all its waste every twenty-three seconds. Still, I could not get just exactly why blood. I knew the Scripture, "Without the shedding of blood, there is no remission of sin" (Heb. 9:22). But I left there wondering why blood is the requirement.

I left Chicago that night and flew to Washington, D.C., to pick up Marilyn, my wife. As we were driving back to Houston, right in the middle of the hills of West Virginia, it hit me like a ton of bricks. Of course, that is the reason Jesus had to die. I said, "Marilyn, write this down as quickly as you can."

Our sin is the ultimate enthroning of self. That is the sin of rebellion. We who are merely men, we make ourselves God. Jesus did exactly the opposite of that. He was God who had made himself a man. And death by the shedding of blood, instead of being the ultimate enthroning of self, is the ultimate denial of self.

And I remember how the Scriptures had said Jesus was faithful even unto the end. "Christ was obedient even unto death" (Phil. 2:8). That is as far as a man could go. Therefore, it only makes sense that we can be forgiven. There *is* power in the *blood* because by shedding his blood, Jesus was in essence reversing our sin, thereby offering *us* forgiveness, peace, and victory.

And this forgiveness is total. It encompasses *all* our sins. When Jesus died on the cross, he died for the sins of the whole world. Right? Right. The sin of every single person after Jesus died on the cross was paid for before the sin was committed. When Jesus died, all of your sins were in the future. God was looking ahead to the future as well as seeing past and present when the way of forgiveness was accomplished. You see, God views all our lives as one big panoramic picture—as one stage, or one setting, one place. When you are in an airplane, many times you can see several cities at one time. This is the same way God views our lives and our sins.

When you really get hold of this in your mind, you will understand how very secure your position is in Christ and how complete is his forgiveness. God doesn't want just to forgive you up to a point at which you can be lost again (if you aren't confessed up to date). Instead, God took your whole life with *all*—I repeat, *all*—its sin and guilt, every single lustful look, adulterous act, covetous feeling that you have ever hidden. Two thousand years before you ever did it, Jesus paid for it. Since God sees all your sins at once as one big panorama, when he receives you into a relationship with himself, he forgives you of the whole thing!

Since that is true, one last question. "Why?" To me, part of the beauty of Almighty God is the magnificant order and design always revealed in him and the heavy purpose and reasoning behind everything he does. Why did Jesus do all this? Why are we forgiven when we don't deserve it? Why does God forgive rather than retaliate? There is a reason. In Psalms 130:4, we get some insight into this. "There is forgiveness with thee that thou may be reverently trusted." "There is forgiveness"—this is the way he accepts us, completely and in spite of all our sin. And the reason is so that we might have a relationship with him of trust.

God wants people that can love him back in the way he loves us. This means nothing between us, no barriers. I mean, let's face it. You can't really love somebody you are "hacked off" with. You can't have a close relationship with somebody you're carrying a grudge for. And you especially can't love someone that you think holds something against you. That is certainly not a relationship of trust. And in the same way, God wants there to be nothing between you and him so you can respond to him in love with respect to his own love.

That's why he wants to forgive you of all your sins. That's why God wants and almost begs you to confess all your sin. He loves you and accepts you as blameless on the basis of your having received Jesus Christ as your Lord and Savior, and he desires a bold, dynamic faith-love

Admit It, Quit It, and Forget It

relationship with you. He wants you to serve him and obey him, not out of duty or for "pie in the sky by and by," but out of thankfulness and love for what he has done in Christ Jesus.

So do you have some sin that is really holding you? Maybe some sexual fling that Satan is using to drive you up the wall? Some sin in the back of your mind that keeps you from having that love-trust relationship with God? If so, admit it, quit it, and forget it. God really means it when he says, "Though your sins be as scarlet, they shall be as white as snow; though they be red like crimson, they shall be as wool" (Isa. 1:18). God, almighty God, has looked beyond your faults and seen your needs.

10

"Get On Your Fatigues"

Recently I was sitting in the team prayer room after the service when two young men about sixteen came walking in quite disturbed and asked to talk privately about something they said was "very important and very personal." As soon as they sat down, it was obvious this was no small problem. One boy continually refused even to look up as the other started out like this: "Well, my friend has a real problem."

"Go ahead."

"Well, you know, last night you were talking about how God takes a definite stand against homosexuality. Well, my friend, he's really got a problem."

I turned to the friend. "What's your name?"

"Bill."

"Bill, you tell me what's happening."

"Well, when I was eleven years old, another boy was spending the night with me. We were looking at some pornographic pictures, and all of a sudden we were on top of each other, and well, you know the rest."

"You were only eleven? Is that the only time you got involved in homosexuality?"

"No. Two other times. But I'm constantly thinking about

it, especially at school. It seems as though even when I really don't want to think about it, I really can't get it out of my mind. I even tell myself I'm not going to think about it any more, but I constantly do, over and over. I just can't seem to stop."

I wish there were some way to adequately describe in this book the war that was going on in this young man's mind. I don't believe I have ever seen a more physical picture of the spiritual warfare which Satan is waging to gain control of our physical lives. It was very obvious that there was a power which took him beyond his own physical desire. That is what the Scripture is talking about when it says, "We wrestle not against flesh and blood [the battle is not just with men or our own physical, sexual desires], but against principalities and powers of darkness." As we talk about temptation, it is expedient that we realize just how real the spiritual world is. Many people never have victory over temptation and never experience the victory Jesus can give. They never realize that the struggle to yield to temptation is beyond that of simply our will-power—"sucking up your guts," "deciding to turn over a new leaf," or even doing better next time.

I remember a guy I questioned just out on the street in California. He was heavy into dope, and as I was talking to him about the Lord, I asked him, "Why are you into this? Why are you blowing your mind? What is it you're really trying to do?" And I remember well his reply. "I'm looking for something outside of myself."

The thing this guy was after is the very thing Satan uses to draw *us* away from God. You look at this life you know and realize there has got to be more than this. So you try everything you can—sex, drugs, popularity, success. But the only place you look is in the physical dimension of life. You've been out for your fling, you've had your sex, you have reached your ten second climax. You finally go home, fall across your own bed and cry out, "There's got to be more than this." But Satan gets you on a merry-go-round. You know there has got to be more, but you don't know where it is. Just as Satan blinds Christians many times to the fulfilling aspects of the spiritual dimension of life found in Jesus, he blinds lost people to the very existence of a spiritual dimension of life.

For the last couple of decades, especially, people have tried to deny the existence of anything spiritual—Jesus, demons, God, the reality of Satan, the whole bit. But in these last few years it has become very evident just how real the spiritual dimension of life is. The Bible very boldly and pointedly says what we are coming to realize today. The real world is not the physical world, but the real world is the spiritual world.

Jesus said in Matthew 10:28, "Don't be afraid of those who can just kill your body, but fear those who can destroy both your body and your soul in hell.' He was simply saying the same thing. The real world, the world that counts the most, is the spiritual world. We become afraid of men when all the time, Satan is the real enemy. And in this spiritual world, God has a master plan for victory—a perfect defense, a perfect offense, plus the promise of victory. As powerful as Satan is, he is no match for Jesus. Praise God! Of course, since God wants real live people and not robots, he won't force himself on anyone. Thus, God's master strategy to overpower Satan works only in the life of the person who has voluntarily surrendered his life to Jesus and has received Jesus as his own personal Lord and Savior.

Here our thinking must be right. The Bible is saying, realize you can't do it yourself. In other words, you cannot defeat Satan and his demons on your own power! If you do not get any other thing out of this book, realize this and understand it. Bring it to the front of your brain: Satan can whip you with his hands tied behind his back. But with Jesus, you can be assured of victory.

One night I was preaching in a small Texas town when one of the football players from the University of Texas accepted Christ. The pastor was so excited about this guy's getting saved that after he had gone through counseling, the pastor brought him back to the church auditorium to give a brief word of testimony. I remember he stood up, probably weighed 250 or 260 pounds, and began his testimony something like this: "Well, when I get back to the University of Texas, I am going to really live for Jesus. I mean I'm really going to do something for Jesus. I'm going to quit all the junk I've been doing. I'm going to talk to the fraternities and I'm going to talk to the sororities and I'm going to tell everybody about Jesus." He was so excited, and everybody there in church applauded and screamed and it was fantastic.

But I knew I had to talk to this guy before he got away. Of course, I was thrilled that he had been saved. But I walked up to him and said, "Jim, if you go back to the University of Texas with that attitude, you'll fall flat on your face." He said, "What do you mean?" "You see Jim, the Christian life is not some sort of super football game.

You can't just suck up your guts and go after it. Just as you were not able to be saved on your own good works and power, in the same way you can't live the Christian life in your own power."

Praise God, Jim left that night realizing that although he was a hunk physically, popular and athletic, the only way he was going to have victory in the Christian experience day by day is through the power and victory of Jesus. This is the place at which so many fail. Victory over sexual temptation will never come in your own strength and power. Turn these temptations over to Jesus and let him take care of them. After all, he's a noted authority on overcoming temptation. In fact, he has set the all-time record for victory.

One of the magnificent things about our Lord Jesus is that he is no "storybook" Savior. It was Jesus who entered into the arena of spiritual warfare and temptation. In the desert, it was Jesus who faced Satan head-on with the restrictions of man and came out victorious.

In fact, it was Jesus in the desert who proved that any Christian really totally depending on the Father for power can defeat Satan. So first turn every part of your life over to Jesus. Ephesians says, "Put on the whole armour of God"—"piecemaking" it will never do. So put it all on "so you can withstand the tricks of the devil" (Eph. 6:11). For you to try to be victorious over Satan without the whole armor of God would be as foolish as a football player trying to be a great player without wearing any pads. He might get in the game, but he would probably be "killed" in the first play.

I remember when I was in junior high as a Freshman,

"Get On Your Fatigues"

I finally got to be on a starting unit on our football team. That was during the days when people were wearing two bars across their helmet as a face guard. Watching pro football for so long on TV, I was always seeing the dazzling quarterback call out the plays with that single bar for a face guard. I chose to go against my coach's judgment to have two bars across my face guard instead of a single one. Well friend, it did not take long to end that. The first game of the season, the second play of the game, somebody hit me right square in the nose right under that single bar face guard. There I was with blood gushing out of my face like a stuck pig; and I will grant you one thing, I put that dual face guard on my helmet.

The very same thing is true in the spiritual world. If we are going to have victory, we are going to have to put on the whole armor. If only one little piece of the armor is missing, it can cost us victory. So remember how important every piece of armor is.

Now, let's look hard at that armor, piece by piece. Ephesians 6:14 says, "Having your loins girt about you with truth!" Almost any Bible teacher will tell you that this phrase refers to the *belt* which is the very foundation garment of the Roman soldier. Every other piece of armor fastened onto the belt. Without it, all the other pieces would fall off. So it is only natural that the belt would be mentioned first. But this is a very special kind of belt, a very special foundation, because it is a belt of *truth!*

When you talk about having victory over Satan, the archdeceiver, it only makes sense that the very basis of that victory will have to be truth. What a time in history to realize this. We're living in a generation that is looking for truth. We've yelled for years now "tell it like it is"—"tell us the truth." But Satan has lied constantly. It only makes sense that Satan would lie. He knows that the truth is the very basis for a person's defense against him. He wants us to believe him, the lie, instead of Jesus, the truth.

There is something about the truth that seems to put everything in perspective. That is what Jesus was saying when he said, "You shall know the truth and the truth shall set you free" (John 8:32). Then he says in John 14:6, "I am the truth." So the very foundation of our victory over Satan is knowing Jesus and giving every area of our life to him. Every other piece of armor finds its foundation in Jesus because he is the truth.

So once you get saved (really turn your life over to Jesus, and receive him as your Lord and Savior), he becomes your foundation; and now you can put on the rest of the armor!

"And having on the breastplate of righteousness." What a fantastic analogy! Realizing we're going to be involved in the middle of a war, Paul says "get on that breastplate!"

In Paul's day, every soldier put on a metal breastplate that protected the vital organs of his body. Today, we need and have that same type of breastplate, but it is the breastplate of righteousness! Now listen closely! At first glance, you could easily mistake what this means. When you first hear the phrase "breastplate of righteousness," you think it probably means that we're supposed to really try to live good and clean, righteous lives. Although this is true, that's not what this Scripture is talking about. This righteousness is not our righteousness, but instead it is the righteousness of Jesus. Amazing! Here we find Jesus is not only our foundation piece of armor, the belt, but his righteousness makes up the covering for the most vital parts of our lives.

There is no doubt that the ancient Roman breastplate was mainly a covering or protection for the heart. Think of the ramifications of this. Our breastplate is the protector for the spiritual heart. The heart in the Bible is not just the "bloodpumper." The spiritual heart is that part of man that responds to God. The heart then, Scripturally, is made up of the emotion, the intellect, and the will. Once again, our breastplate is the protector of the vital areas of our lives. Jesus is the protector of our emotion, our will, and our intellect, guarding us from Satan.

So many times, we are caught without our breastplate on. Satan comes to tell us how wicked and perverse we are. He convinces us we're so weak, that we continually fail. He's right. We are! In fact, the Bible says (Isa. 64:6) that "our righteousnesses are as filthy rags." But Satan never tells us that. Instead he wants us to try to rely upon our own good works. Then he depresses and overcomes us when we can't produce the righteousness we're never supposed to produce to begin with. Satan wants to keep the battle between you and him. He wants Jesus left out of the battle because he knows Jesus would win!

In the area of sex, this is no less true. You promise yourself a million times you really want to stay pure, but you don't. Why? Because so many of you are trying to make it against Satan in your righteousness, your strength, and your willpower, instead of allowing Jesus to win over the temptation for you. You aren't using your breastplate. You are going into battle without part of your armor. No wonder you lose. You are leaving your emotion, will, and intellect open to an attack from Satan. The righteousness of Jesus has got to be your breastplate.

The old Roman breastplates were layers thick—so is yours. You see, it is Jesus—his life, our example—making up a part of the breastplate. It is Jesus—his Word, the Bible, your guide, your rule book—making up a part of the breastplate. It's Jesus—his Spirit, the Holy Spirit—in control of your life. His power giving another layer of covering to the breastplate. No dart or spear, no trick of Satan, can get through that breastplate of Jesus. When Satan is attacking your emotions, intellect, and will, Jesus is there to give you power to make Satan flee.

"And your feet shod with the preparation of the gospel of peace" (Eph. 6:15).

There are so many analogies to draw here that it almost blows your mind. I mean, let's face it. Nothing is more important to a soldier, especially in the day of the Bible, than his feet. Almost every soldier was in the infantry. He could have all the armor on just right; but if he couldn't stand up and fight, he was useless as a soldier. I remember in playing football how so many times one little blister would keep a guy from really performing his best. But this means more than just putting on a few "spiritual Dr.Scholl's pads" and having your sandals nice and shiny. The key phrases in this verse are "preparation" and "the gospel of peace."

Now think! Satan brings to the battleground (your mind) thousands of years of experience and supernatural, cunning might. If you think you can haphazardly walk into the battlefield and be victorious, you are on the ultimate ego trip of history. You are going to have to learn to do spiritual.

warfare. You must get prepared. But not with just any type of preparation. It must be the preparation of "the gospel of peace." This *does* mean time in Bible study, learning the messages and doctrine of the Scriptures so that you do not waver, so that you will not be easily seduced by "doctrines of devils" (1 Tim. 4:1). But beyond that, "the gospel of peace" means the gospel of assurance. In other words, our whole being is to be firmly planted and rest firm upon a foundation of *assurance*. Here again it is Jesus! He now becomes our footing.

How else could we face the strength of Satan without turning and running or simply yielding? The only way is that we are assured of our salvation and know without a doubt that it is Jesus' power with which we face the world and Satan. With confidence we're ready for any temptation that the devil can come up with, knowing the victory is *already* ours. What Satan wants is to get us on shaky ground, to get us where we've lost our footing, our assurance of our salvation and Jesus' power. Then he can move in and attack us without opposition.

"Above all, taking the shield of faith wherewith ye shall be able to quench all the fiery darts of the wicked!" (Eph. 6:16).

I know this is trite. I almost hate to say it, because I know in many cases it is going to run in one ear and out the other. But if you'll get this, you really can have victory!

When you get saved, when you surrender your life to Jesus, he comes into your life and forgives you and cleanses you of your sin. Then by the person of the Holy Spirit, he comes to live in your life. At that point, he becomes your victory, your power, your love, your joy, your strength, everything. He becomes your armor, your breastplate, shield, sword, helmet, everything!

But, if you do not have *faith* in him to *be* these things—although he *is* all of these things—you make his power to give you victory noneffective in your life. When you are trusting Jesus, there is nothing in any way that Satan can do to you, no trick he can come up with, no new strategy he can plan, that Jesus can't overcome. All the power of God, all of it, is available to you at the flick of the switch of faith!

First John 5:4 says, "This is the victory that overcomes the world, faith, even our faith." No sucking up your guts, not doing your best—*faith!* Until you really have faith in God, you'll never put on any of the armor. This is why God says, *"above all,* have faith." And Galatians 2:20 goes on to explain that Jesus even supplies the faith! In fact, it's his faith. "And the life which I now live in the flesh I live by the *faith of the Son of God,* who loved me and gave himself for me." Once again, it's Jesus! As we become one with him, his faith becomes our faith.

If you feel short on faith, ask Jesus. "Ye have not because ye ask not" (James 4:2). And delve into the Scriptures and allow him to speak back to you and reveal himself. "Faith cometh by hearing and hearing by the word of God." So put up that shield of faith and trust Jesus to be all that he is. Now *act* on your faith, and go forward. This is your victory!

"And take the helmet of salvation, and the sword of the Spirit, which is the Word of God" (Eph. 6:17). Watch this. Every piece of armor thus far has been defensive. Now there are offensive weapons. Number one, your salvation. It may seem odd that your salvation becomes an offensive tool. But that's because it establishes your position in regard to Satan and the world. "But God is so rich in mercy; he loved us so much that even though we were spiritually dead and doomed by our sins, he gave us back our lives again when he raised Christ from the dead (Only by his undeserved favor have we ever been saved), and lifted us up from the grave into glory along with Christ, where we sit with him in the heavenly realms . . . all because of what Christ Jesus did" (Eph. 2:4-7). Spiritually, being one with Christ Jesus, we are already at the right hand of God with the world at our feet. If you've really given your life to Jesus and thereby become a Christian, every demon in hell and Satan himself is under your control. You can demand in the name of Jesus that Satan and his demons leave your mind. Because of your "position" as a believer, the Scriptures declare they must go!

Then you have your sword—the Bible, the Word of God. Drive Satan out of your mind and thoughts with the written Word of God! The Bible itself tells us that it is a two-edged sword. The Romans were the smarties that came up with the two-edged sword. It was smaller, but much more powerful. It wouldn't swing a soldier off balance, and little time for turning was involved since the blade could "fell a victim" in either direction.

The Word of God works just this way. If hidden in our hearts, it keeps Satan from catching us off balance. And it works two-edgedly. It not only drives Satan's lies and suggestions from our minds, but it goes further to strengthen and renew us by filling our minds up with God's truths.

So here you are, a completely dressed and ready-to-go soldier. But beyond that, because of the fact that Jesus defeated Satan at the cross, we already know who is going to win the battle—Jesus! He is our ultimate defense, our armor. He is our offense, our weapon. He is our victory!

So cheer up and remember this is no dress rehearsal, this is the real thing. The war is raging, so get in the battle! The victory is yours.

But one last word of caution: Even with all your armor on, the devil is still a tricky advisary and will try anything to get to you, so be on the lookout for him. Rely on Jesus.

11

It's Worth Waiting For!

How well I remember the temptations I've mentioned in this book because I *faced most of them* personally. I know from personal experience that Satan would like to destroy every person with the biggest temptation of all—*sex*. But I also know that Jesus, through his Holy Spirit, can give you victory over Satan and the temptation of sex because he has done it in *my life!*

I remember from grade school how we would go over to someone's home after school and have our little parties as we listened and danced to American Bandstand. Someone always came up with the idea of playing spin-the-bottle or post office, and off we'd go on our "make-out" times for the next hour or so. With that beginning, Satan launched a continuing struggle for the supremacy of my mind in the area of sex.

When I was thirteen, I remember being at a party—the regular little junior-high party. After dancing with a girl quite a while, a girl who I then thought *had* to be the one for me, the two of us walked outside to the parking lot. As we stood there talking, she took my hands, and for the next few minutes the devil tried hard to teach me how much fun petting could be. Don't let anybody kid you. The devil doesn't always come disguised as a man.

At the age of sixteen, Satan pulled out all the stops. He brought me extremely close to adultery! I thought I was so in love with this girl that nothing else in the world mattered! I thought I literally couldn't go on living without her! I know that sounds melodramatic—but those were the exact thoughts running through my mind. (And most people have been there at some time.) In fact, I wanted her so much that even though she was married, the devil still almost used that desire to destroy what the Lord had in store for my life. The only thing that kept me from doing what my lust wanted to do was my love for Jesus Christ.

That moment was one of the key experiences in my Christian growth. It was with that temptation that God proved to me he could give me victory over any temptation I would ever face. Through a great youth director, a wonderful Christian adult friend, and an understanding, loving Dad, God had brought me to a point of realization. What he had in store for me was ten thousand times more important than a moment of sexual bliss which would have destroyed me for the kingdom's use. So instead of yielding, I resisted Satan through Jesus' power.

Then things really began to happen! It was as though God saw that I was willing to resist Satan in the area of sex, then started opening up the doors for me to sing all over the place and share Jesus on an unbelievable scale! It was as though God brought me to a certain point of maturity by testing me; then, seeing that I wasn't going to sell out for the devil's temporary pleasure, he really started using me.

It's Worth Waiting For!

Almost immediately after that God started laying the foundation for the terrific—beautiful—marriage with my wife, Marilyn. We had a fantastic time together. We got unbelievably high on Jesus together! I can honestly say that I fell in love with my wife before I ever even kissed her! And because of the previous experience in resisting Satan in that area, God gave us victory over sex in our date life. He showed us that a real love relationship involves so much more than just a craving for each other's body.

Because we were willing to let God really have control of our lives as Christian teen-agers (and only because of that), my wife and I walked the aisle pure—pure before God *and* man. Oh, we heard all the devil's ole excuses for why we should experience premarital sex. One guy even told us we wouldn't know what we were doing when we got married—we wouldn't know *how* if we didn't experiment around some first (maybe with someone else who knew). Well, gang, he was right! He was so right! We didn't know a thing when we got married—but what a fantastic joy to see God lead us completely in this area as he has in so many others.

I was preaching in Hamilton, Ohio, and made the statement one evening, "It's worth waiting for."

Afterwards a boy came up to me and said, "Preacher, I don't mean this to be smart-alecky, but *why* is it worth waiting for?"

Well, let me give you seven reasons why I *know* it's worth waiting for:

1) *Just knowing that when we walked down the aisle we both began our marriage pure sexually; we were both virgins!*

How *great* it was to know that the white gown my wife wore was not a joke—not a farce—that she had actually saved herself for me. And how fantastic it was to know that she was not getting a secondhand deal either, because I had saved myself for her.

2) *It's worth waiting for just to be able to always have complete trust in each other!* Marilyn and I have said so often, in reviewing other people's problems, "How unreal it is! How hard it is to imagine! Why, *I* never think of anyone but you. And I never feel that you think of anyone else either." Trust is the most important point in our marriage (or any marriage). And how important that is, especially in the ministry. When I have to be away somewhere preaching, I can honestly say that I never even *think* of Marilyn's being unfaithful to me. I know she kept herself pure for me *before* marriage. Therefore, I know how much more she will keep herself for me *inside* of our marriage.

3) *Not having to worry about disease that could cripple us or our children makes it worth waiting for.* Enough said! Without sex before marriage there is no possibility of it— and no fear!

4) *Not having any bad memories and guilt feelings makes it worth waiting for.* When you wait, it's perfect—as God intended it. You have no secrets to keep. You can be totally committed to that one person—unashamedly and unreservedly! You haven't allowed any dirt to get in—to warp your view or mar your present experience—nothing to sweep under the rug before you can enjoy all that God has arranged for you!

5) *Being able to share with others that Jesus can give you the victory makes it worth waiting for.* I'm so glad that

when my child counts from the date of his birth back to the date of my marriage I won't have to make explanations. And even if a child is not born early, many times he inquires of his parents about their own premarital standards and relations. I'm not going to have to be embarrassed or lie. Instead, I can share with him the victory which Christ gave me and can likewise give to him.

I've met so many kids embittered toward their parents and with no respect for them at all. And I've met so many parents who shake their heads over their children's troubles and say, "Well, we set the example. What else could we expect?" Marilyn and I have some newly married friends, and they are already worried about what they will say fifteen years from now—what will they tell their child?

Admittedly, it is even more important in my work to be able to share this victory. But even if I weren't in the ministry, it would be of utmost importance to me *just because I'm a Christian.* I want to be that example, that light to a crooked and perverse nation and to the world (Phil. 2:15). I couldn't have written this book if God hadn't given me victory. Quite frankly, it was worth waiting for just so I can tell you that it is *possible* with God. Christ *can* give you victory!

6) *Getting to learn sex together makes it worth waiting for.* Sex is a fantastic wonderful adventure that gets better and better when done within the confines of marriage as God planned it. When sex is shared in marriage with the one you loved even *without sex,* that makes the completion of sex a billion times more enjoyable and precious.

7) *Most of all, it's worth waiting for just to know that you are pure before God.* In this book I've shown you reasons

why as a true Jesus person you need to keep yourself pure. But if everything else I said were invalid (I said, *"If"*), the fact that God says, "Thou shalt not commit adultery," is all the authority that should be needed for you to keep your purity intact.

Now, if you reject God—if you don't accept Jesus as being his only begotten Son—then naturally there's no reason for your keeping yourself pure except for some of the practical ones mentioned. If there is no God—if Jesus is a joke—then there is no moral code or eternal life, and you *ought* to act like an animal and "get all you can while the gettin's good!"

But if you have really turned your life over to Jesus—if you have voluntarily committed your will to the will of God—you have been *chosen* to be a Christian. And if for no other reason, you must keep yourself pure because *God demands it!*